CAREERS AFTER THE ARMED FORCES

The greater danger for most of us
lies not in setting our aim too high
and falling short; but in setting our
aim too low, and achieving our mark.

Michelangelo

CAREERS AFTER THE ARMED FORCES

How to decide on
the right career and make
a successful transition

Jon Mitchell

KOGAN PAGE

London and Philadelphia

Publisher's note

Every possible effort has been made to ensure that the information contained in this book is accurate at the time of going to press, and the publishers and authors cannot accept responsibility for any errors or omissions, however caused. No responsibility for loss or damage occasioned to any person acting, or refraining from action, as a result of the material in this publication can be accepted by the editor, the publisher or any of the authors.

First published in Great Britain and the United States in 2009 by Kogan Page Limited

Kogan Page Limited
120 Pentonville Road
London N1 9JN
United Kingdom
www.koganpage.com

525 South 4th Street, #241
Philadelphia PA 19147
USA

© Jon Mitchell, 2009

ISBN 978 0 7494 5530 9

British Library Cataloguing-in-Publication Data

A CIP record for this book is available from the British Library.

Library of Congress Cataloging-in-Publication Data

Mitchell, Jon.
  Careers after the Armed Forces : how to decide on the right career and make a successful transition / Jon Mitchell. -- 1st ed.
    p. cm.
  Includes bibliographical references.
  ISBN 978-0-7494-5530-9
  1. Vocational guidance. 2. Occupations. 3. Armed Forces. I. Title.
  HF5381.M556 2009
  650.14--dc22
                              2009008500

Typeset by Jean Cussons Typesetting, Diss, Norfolk
Printed and bound in India by Replika Press Pvt Ltd

Contents

Foreword

Whatever your rank, leaving the Services is a challenge. Jon has put together a very readable book which explains clearly the processes and pitfalls. In an evermore competitive world, decide what you want from your second career, understand how to communicate your skills and experience and unashamedly develop and use your networks. The best of luck.

Major General M S White CB CBE JP

About the author

Jon Mitchell is a certified Career Coach and a member of the International Coach Federation.

He has a background in Marketing and ran his own successful recruitment consultancy before selling the business and moving full time into Coaching.

Jon is a Career Transition Coach and works with professional people from a variety of backgrounds. The focus of his work is in helping people who are looking for clarity around the future direction of their career.

He particularly wants to help people who are unhappy in their career, because he has been there personally. He spent a long time working in a career he really didn't enjoy and having found a career that he is truly passionate about he wants to help others achieve the same goal.

Jon has been working with Armed Forces leavers for a number of years and understands the unique challenges they face.

For more information about Jon, please visit his website at www.jonmitchell.co.uk or e-mail him at jon@jonmitchell.co.uk.

Acknowledgements

Little Tin. Thank you for always being there and for giving us two amazing boys.

A big thank you also to Marianne and Firework Career Coaching for influencing my coaching in such a positive way and allowing me to use one of their exercises as the basis for the Careers Bank exercise in the book.

Introduction

This book has been written with a focus on people within the commissioned ranks as well as the middle- to senior non-commissioned ranks, but I would hope it would be useful to any person who is considering leaving the Armed Forces.

The aim of the book is simple – to help people who are considering leaving the Armed Forces to answer some fundamental questions. Should I leave the Forces? Is now the right time to leave? What am I going to do when I leave? Will I enjoy it? How will I get the right job?

How the book endeavours to do this is by helping to work out what the ideal career is, reality-checking it, then developing a realistic action plan of how to get there. The book also provides some useful resources to help get through the transition.

Fundamentally, if you are looking to leave the Armed Forces you need to do some long hard thinking in terms of what's important to you, what makes you tick, and then apply specific career ideas to that.

Working in the Armed Forces, wherever in the world, is a truly unique experience. People often face life and death situations and, as a result, very strong bonds develop between people 'at work' – bonds that often don't develop to such an extent 'at work' in the civilian world.

Also, work and social lives can be heavily intertwined, with family and partners often living on bases and being very much part of military life.

As a result, leaving this all behind (even if it may form some of the reason for your decision to leave) may create some real doubts and fears, potentially clouding judgement at a critical time.

The book aims to alleviate some of these natural concerns by helping to answer the key questions posed at the beginning of this introduction.

By getting clarity, understanding and awareness around what is going to be the right career direction for you and then developing a detailed and realistic action plan of how to get there, I would hope that your concerns and worries would be reduced... they aren't going to disappear completely until you have actually made the change and are happy in your new role.

More broadly speaking, the key belief I hold around careers and what underlies my coaching is: Find your true passion, success will follow and rewards in turn will follow that (often including financial ones!).

So many people come to me looking at the situation, in my view, in completely the wrong way – they are chasing the money first and foremost. They are focusing on the wrong outcome and unless they are very fortunate and stumble across a real passion, they won't be truly happy in their work long term, even if they do earn a lot of money! I'm sure you've come across people who seem to have so much, all 'the goodies' and yet aren't happy… It's no wonder so many people are unhappy in their jobs.

Now, I'm not a complete idealist – I'm not saying money isn't an important part of the equation, we all have mortgages and bills to pay. I'm just saying don't let it be your primary goal. Don't forget this, find your true passion and it will give you direction, a path to start down and something to strive for.

Generally, I don't find this financial issue to be the case with Forces leavers because money is often low on the list of reasons most people join the Forces in the first place. However, this can gain greater importance when looking for a role in the commercial world, so please do bear it in mind.

Changing career can be an extremely challenging, stressful and time-consuming process, but if you are committed and determined to make the changes and plan accordingly I am sure you will succeed.

One of the big advantages you have as a potential Forces leaver is time and support. The time and support you have will depend on your country, rank and length of service, but mostly you will have a longer time to find the right job than you would if you were moving from one role to another in the commercial sector.

Also the support given by the Armed Forces for leavers can be extremely beneficial including free or subsidized university degrees and MBAs. Again, this varies from country to country, and length of service and rank, but the support can be extremely beneficial, so please make sure you are completely aware of the support available to you and make good use of it.

It may not come as a surprise to you but due to the length/ frequency of tours and the dangers involved, more Armed Forces personnel in a number of countries are now considering leaving than ever before – for example, in the UK it has recently been widely reported that nearly 50 per cent* of Armed Forces personnel are considering leaving... a staggering amount, and I'm sure the UK is not alone in this.

Whichever country you are in, if you are considering leaving the Armed Forces you need to ensure you take full advantage of the time and resources available to you and plan an effective and smooth transition.

The book is interactive and there are a number of chapters that include exercises and questions posed, so you may want to get a pen and paper to hand before you begin reading.

At the beginning of the book I have deliberately focused on self-reflection and self-analysis, with the later stages of the book focusing on providing practical tips and advice.

Some of you may view the self-analysis section of the book as being 'a bit fluffy'. I know that, because having worked with a number of Forces leavers over the years there is sometimes some initial resistance to this type of work. However, this is a key part of the process in terms of stretching you and getting you to think in new ways. This section will help you work out what is going to be the right career for you and make the transition as painless as possible, so please do read it and work on the exercises.

Also, I've looked to keep the exercises as simple and concise as possible as I've found that so many exercises can get complicated and can muddy the water rather than give clarity as intended. When looking to complete the exercises I would

_____

(* Oct 2007 UK Ministry of Defence Survey found that 47 per cent of the Army and Royal Navy and 44 per cent of the Royal Air Force were considering leaving)

recommend reading the book through first. I would hope you find it an inspiring read and that it will give you added motivation and understanding to complete the exercises effectively.

Some of the exercises are available to download from the internet. Please see the Kogan Page website, www.koganpage.com, and my website, www.jonmitchell.co.uk, for more information. There are also some blank 'Notes' pages at the back of the book for you to use.

I hope you enjoy the book and find it thought provoking.

Jon

Part 1

Evaluating your current career situation

1

Career and life health check

A good starting point when considering changing career is to evaluate and reflect on where you are with your career at the moment and, on a larger scale, your life in general.

It's important to consider your life as a whole, as your career and life are intertwined – you spend so much time working that if you don't enjoy it, it can have a knock-on effect on the other areas of your life.

Please use the Work and Life Charts (Figures 1.1 and 1.3) to help evaluate where you are at the moment.

How to use the charts

On the Work Chart, for each area of your working life give yourself a score from 1 to 10 on your level of satisfaction (with 10 being great, couldn't be better and 1 being I hope it doesn't get any worse!).

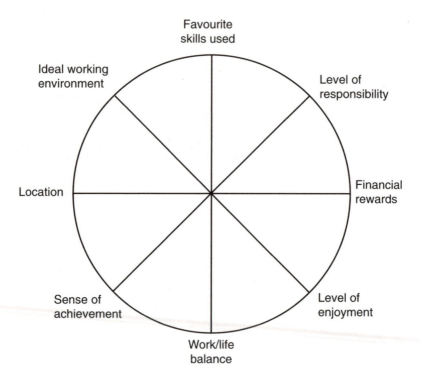

Figure 1.1

Key questions to ask yourself

■ How much have I enjoyed the work I have done over the last 12 months?

■ How happy have I been with the level of responsibility I have had?

■ What has my work and home life balance been like?

■ What level of achievement and satisfaction have I had from my work when I look back over the years?

■ How happy have I been with my working environment? This can include the physical environment, the people I work with etc.

■ How happy am I with the location of my work? Is it city based, town, field based etc? Do I enjoy working in that type of location?

■ What are the key skills I have been using? Are these skills I enjoy using?

■ What has the level of my financial reward been like for all my hard work during the year?

Once you have a score for each area, plot it out on the circle with zero being at the centre and 10 being at the outer edge.

To get an overall picture of the balance in your working life simply connect the dots. Figure 1.2 shows an example of a completed Work Chart.

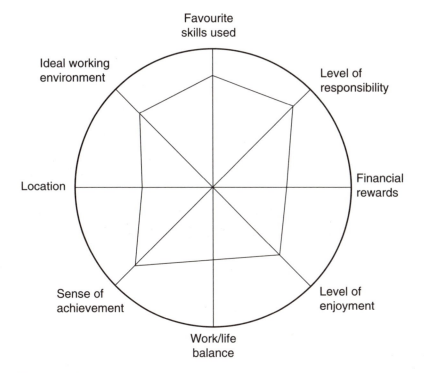

Figure 1.2

Use the same scoring system when completing your Life Chart (Figure 1.3).

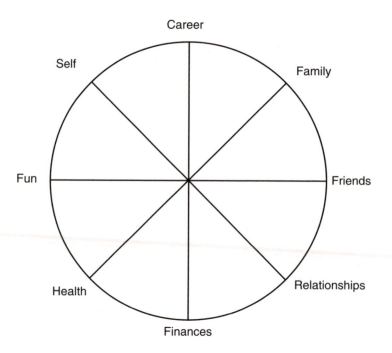

Figure 1.3

Analysing the Work and Life Charts

Key questions you need to ask yourself once you have completed the Work and Life Charts are the following:

1. If the charts you have developed were 'wheels', how big would your wheels be? The bigger the wheel the better.

2. If these were actual wheels on your car, how smooth would the ride be?
3. What can you do now to increase the size of your wheels and smooth out the ride?

So, what are your thoughts on your work and life wheels? What areas would you like to develop? Write down any initial ideas you have in the space below.

Ideas

_____

_____

_____

_____

_____

_____

_____

_____

_____

_____

_____

Evaluating your current work/life balance

A lot of Armed Forces are currently under a lot of pressure in terms of stretched resources. This, combined with the pressures of day to day modern life means that work/life balance is one key aspect a lot of Armed Forces people struggle with and I would like to spend a few minutes focusing on this.

As part of the Work Chart exercise (Figure 1.1) you will have scored yourself for work/life balance. If you put a low score against it, what was the reason?

I know Forces life is unique and there are some things you don't have any control over, especially length and frequency of tours, but as John's story later in the chapter shows, changes can be made.

Use the following questions to help you consider the possible reasons and changes you can make:

- **Where are you going wrong?** What is stopping you from getting the right balance?

■ **What is the ideal situation for you?** How will you know when you have achieved it? How will you feel when you have achieved it? What will you be doing? (Create as vivid and detailed a picture of this as possible – this will really help to motivate you to achieve the changes.)

■ **What have you done so far to achieve a better balance in your life?** What changes do you still need to make? (Make a complete list.) What has stopped you from making these changes so far?

John's story

John was a recently promoted Major in the Army. Up to the point where John came to see me he had recently done two tours of Iraq and one of Afghanistan... and was both physically and mentally exhausted.

As he described to me, up until recently the Army had been his life and he had absolutely loved it. The long and varied tours had always been part of the enjoyment and he had craved the excitement and variety the Army offered him.

His goal for the last few years had been to be promoted to Major. However, now he had been promoted, he started to question his motives.

One of the things John was questioning was his work/life balance. He had recently got married and realized he no longer wanted to be away from home so much. In the longer term John realized he wanted to leave the Army and in the short term he wanted to be at home more so he could spend more time with his wife and also have the time to plan his exit strategy from the Army.

By talking to his Commanding Officer about roles that may be available to him as a recently promoted Major it became apparent there was a liaison role available which would mean being based near to home and where he would work regular hours.

John has just moved into this new role and having recently talked to him, his enthusiasm, energy and motivation levels are really high again. It takes him 15 minutes to drive to work and he is working normal hours, Monday to Friday with weekends off.

Also, he now has the time to decide on a future career direction and is putting his plan into practice.

Final Note

Often it is a lack of understanding or clarity of where the problem lies, that is the difficulty in creating the right work/life balance.

Yes, it can be extremely challenging getting the right work/life balance when working in the Armed Forces as you often have limited control over where and when you are posted and the hours you need to work… but the key here is that if you feel that this lack of control is becoming a real challenge for you, then you need to consider why that's the case and what you can do to change it.

We all have choices and no matter what the reason is behind you having a poor work/life balance, you **can** choose to change it. Yes, it may take time to put the changes in place, but you can do it.

One of the things I get my clients to consider if they are struggling to make a change is to imagine they are on their deathbed reflecting back on their life. If you were to consider where you are right now with your career, what would you advise yourself to do? What changes would you advise yourself to make?

Good luck with your changes. Life is too short not to get the right balance.

'Regret for things we did can be tempered by time; it is regret for the things we did not do that is inconsolable.'

Sydney J Harris

Possible reasons to consider leaving the Armed Forces

So you are contemplating leaving the Armed Forces. Below are a number of aspects to consider when looking to make a decision.

General unhappiness

Are you suffering from the Sunday night blues? Do you feel low at the end of your leave, knowing you are back at work the next day? Do you count down the time left before you have to go back to work? Are you struggling to get motivated when at work? Are you lacking energy or generally 'not being yourself'?

Enthusiasm and belief

How positive do you feel about the work you are doing? Do you find yourself talking enthusiastically about it or are you disillusioned by it?

10–15 years' time

Can you see yourself being in the Armed Forces in 10–15 years' time? How does it make you feel?

Look back

Look back at the time you have spent in the Armed Forces. How much have you enjoyed it? If it hasn't been particularly enjoyable at times, what stopped you from enjoying it? How much have you progressed? If you are not happy with the way things have progressed, what's stopped you?

Square peg in a round hole?

Are you the right type of person for the Armed Forces? How well do you get on with your colleagues? Do you have similar beliefs and values?

This takes real honesty to admit, but are you in this situation? If you are, be honest with yourself now and make changes because sooner or later it will catch up with you.

Final Note

No one else can decide what is going to be the right career for you, no matter how well you feel they know you – you must take on the responsibility and decide for yourself.

Review how happy you are and become aware of what is particularly important to you. Once you have clarity around this, it will be much easier to make a judgement call on what is going to be the right career for you moving forwards.

Part 2

Deciding on the right career

So you're considering leaving the Armed Forces, but what career is going to be right for you? In Part 2 we will look at getting more clarity around what is going to be the right career for you moving forwards.

As we mentioned in Part 1, it is important to consider your life as a whole and not just your work. With that in mind Part 2 is split into key work and key life considerations.

If you have been in the Armed Forces all your working life, it can be challenging to answer all the questions that may arise, as you haven't had exposure or experience of anything else. However, based on what you know and where you are in your life now, answer them as thoroughly and accurately as possible.

Things can change – and may indeed do so – as you get experience of new ways of working. But you need a starting point, and you can work that out based on the experience you have to date. Please make a note of your findings as you go through this section of the book, as we will refer to them later on.

Key work considerations

Firstly let's consider your key work considerations and what's important to you in the workplace. There is a summary chart (Table 4.4) at the end of this chapter to record your thoughts.

Ideal working environment

What type of environment would you love to work in? Table 4.1 highlights various environments.

Go through the table and make a note of your preferred environments. Then narrow your list down to the three aspects that are most important to you.

Table 4.1

Indoors or outdoors		Travelling – home, abroad, none	
Office-based or based in the field		Creative or practical work	
Working from home		Smart or casual dress	
City/town/village/ countryside based		Open-plan or individual offices	
Owner of business, co-owner or employee		Lively atmosphere or quiet/considered	
Large/medium/ small/one man band business		Fast or gentle-paced work	
Head of a team, part of a team or working alone		Cutting edge or traditional business	
Full time, part time, portfolio career (number of different careers), consultancy		Other:	
Hierarchical or flat- flat-structured organization		Other:	
Like-minded or a diverse group of people		Other:	

Work motivators

What are the things that motivate you the most in the workplace? Use the list of work motivators (Table 4.2) to help you.

For each work motivator, score it on a scale of 1–10, with 10 being of utmost importance to you and 1 being of little importance. Once you have done that, pick out the three work motivators that are of greatest importance to you.

Table 4.2

Status		Competing		Physical challenge		Opportunities available	
Responsibility		Recognition		Inspiring others		Risk-taking	
Intellectual challenge		Variety of work		Autonomy		Producing best product/ product	
Financial remuneration		Financial security		Making a real difference		Making changes	
Achievement		Making something		Learning and development		Job security	
Creativity		Teamwork		Being appreciated		Location	
Integrity		Independence		Helping others		Trust	
Work/life balance		Leadership		The people		Other:	
Fun		Leaving a legacy		Being my own boss		Other:	
Freedom		Advancement		Progressive		Other:	
Relaxed atmosphere		Enjoyment		Profession-alism		Other:	

Favourite work skills

What are the work skills you have and, importantly, that you enjoy using? Use Table 4.3 to help you.

Again, score each aspect on a scale of 1–10 and then pick out your top three.

Table 4.3

Problem solving		People development		Facilitating		Researching	
Negotiating		Public speaking		Delegating		Painting	
Taking on responsibility		Diplomacy		Running a business		Writing	
Completing tasks		Influencing		Organizing		Designing	
Project management		Brain-storming		Entrepre-neurship		Drawing	
Teamwork		Relationship building		Advising		Other:	
Meeting deadlines		Communi-cating		Administra-tion		Other:	
People management		Leading		Analysing		Other:	
Identifying and organizing tasks		Planning		Budgeting		Other:	

Professional strengths

Focus on your key professional strengths. What are they? Ask two or three key people you work with or have worked with what they feel are your key professional strengths.

Examples of professional strengths could be: working well under pressure, lateral thinking, having empathy, being innovative etc. Narrow the list down to your top three.

Ideal working day

If you could spend a typical working day doing anything, what would it be? What skills would you be using? Who would you be working with? What else? Put down your top three thoughts.

This is about what you would **ideally** love to do, so please include the things you would really love to do, no matter how far fetched they may seem.

What I truly want from my career is...

Look back through all the above work considerations you have noted down. Now make a summary of five or six key things you want from your career to truly enjoy it – the most important aspects for you.

Mark's story

Mark had been flying Apache helicopters for a number of years. He had become disillusioned with his work but couldn't decide what he wanted to do with his career.

When we first met he was extremely downcast and negative. I asked him what he liked about his job and he went through a long list of things he didn't like. I asked him again what he did like and he initially couldn't think of anything! He was so focused on what he didn't like and the negative aspects of his work but had little understanding of what he actually did like about his job.

By breaking Mark's work considerations down into the key components using this exercise he was able to focus on individual aspects rather than the broader picture. By doing this, the things that were important to Mark about his work became much clearer, and as a result he became much more positive and motivated.

Final Note

By considering the above key areas you will build up a strong and detailed picture of what is important to you in the work environment.

It is only once you have a clear idea of what it is you would love to do, that you can begin to work towards it.

People reach a point where they are so unhappy with their work they focus on what they don't like about their work, and little time on what they do actually like. Even if you absolutely hate your current job, there will be aspects that you like, even if you have to search hard to find them.

Summary of key work considerations

Table 4.4

Work considerations	Details
Ideal working environment	1. 2. 3.
Work motivators	1. 2. 3.
Favourite work skills	1. 2. 3.
Professional strengths	1. 2. 3.
Ideal working day	1. 2. 3.
What I truly want from my career is…	1. 2. 3. 4. 5. 6.

5

Key 'life' considerations

Next, let's consider the bigger picture, your life outside of work. Again, please make a note of your findings. There is a summary chart (Table 5.2) at the end of the chapter to record your findings.

Your personality type

I've put this down first because knowing and understanding your own personality type can help in understanding who you are and what is going to make you happy.

There are a huge number of personality profiling tools out there and it can be a bit of a minefield choosing the right one and ensuring you are getting benefit from it. As a standalone exercise some profiling tools can be misleading, especially if interpreted wrongly. However, when added to a mix of exercises they can be a very effective resource.

I use a simple Myers-Briggs online assessment with my clients as it gives an accurate profile of your personality type and the top-line can be easy to interpret. Myers-Briggs is based on the psychological types originally described by Carl Jung and is proven to be both a valid and reliable tool. More than two million people worldwide take the test every year.

The test can be done at www.personalitypage.com, for a small fee. Once you have completed the test, draw out what you feel are the three key points from the profile that are of greatest importance to you and include them in the summary chart (Table 5.2).

Part of the report offers career suggestions that may be of interest to your personality type – please keep a note of any career suggestions that interest you and refer to them when considering your Careers Bank exercise later in the book.

For those that find this tool particularly powerful there are qualified Myers-Briggs assessors who can assess your results in greater detail. Please see the Appendix for further details.

Personal interests

The things that you are passionate about and have a real interest in can sometimes help to gain some insight into an area of work that you may enjoy.

Beware; sometimes when an interest becomes a career, the interest wanes – try it first to make sure this isn't going to happen to you.

How do you use your leisure time? What would you rather be doing? What are you passionate about now? What inspires you these days?

Make a note of your top three interests in the summary chart (Table 5.2).

Personal strengths

Being aware of your key personal strengths is important in understanding what you are good at and enjoy doing.

A good way of clarifying what your key personal strengths are is to ask two or three people (non-work-related people) who you respect to tell you what they believe are your three greatest strengths.

Before you do, write down what you believe are your three greatest strengths and compare them to the responses you get.

Examples of personal strengths could be reliable, entertaining, humorous, empathetic, supportive etc.

Narrow the lists down to your top three personal strengths and add them to the summary chart (Table 5.2).

Personal achievements

Your key achievements will give you a clear indication of the type of things you enjoy doing outside of work and whether any could be applied to a work environment.

What are the three personal achievements to date that you are most proud of? What was it that you enjoyed specifically? What is it about them that are important to you?

The achievements you consider don't need to be big, grand achievements. The key is that they are important achievements to you. Add your top three achievements to the summary chart (Table 5.2).

Your core values

Our values are an extremely important consideration and are the foundations or building blocks of who we are. They are the elements we consciously or subconsciously refer to when making decisions in our lives. As Smith (2000, pp38/77) explains, they are 'what we believe to be of greatest importance and of highest priority in our lives.'

> Personal values are the core of our personality and play a large part in unifying our behaviours. They are something we instinctively move towards prompted from within. Our values influence the way we respond to people and events, direct and motivate us towards certain goals and even influence our choice of career and partners.
>
> Zeus, P and Skiffington, S (2000)

It is important that your core values are being honoured as you may ultimately become unhappy if they are being dishonoured. When you become clear of your core values, it can have a hugely beneficial impact when making key decisions in your life such as changing career.

If, for example, you are going to be working for a company or individuals with particularly strong values, it is important that your values are aligned otherwise long-term it is unlikely you will be happy there. Yes, you can adapt your style of work to fit in there, but if your values aren't aligned it will cause difficulties for you in the long-term.

Most of us are roughly aware of what our core values are – loyalty, honesty, integrity etc – but often we aren't exactly clear which of these values are of utmost importance to us. A number of my clients, when we initially look at values, feel that everyone has pretty much the same core values.

Having elicited values with a lot of clients now, I can tell you that really isn't the case. People's core values do vary considerably and by getting clarity around your own core values it can help you considerably.

Also I have noticed that Forces leavers often have extremely strong values around such things as loyalty, friendship and honour. A number of organizations pay lip service to these types of values being of utmost importance to them when, if I put my cynical hat on, they may not in reality be that important to them.

That certainly isn't always the case, but what I'm saying is that if these types of values are that important to you, ensure as much as you can that the organization and people you work with in civilian life have similar values. This, I am sure, is one of the reasons why Forces people can be attracted to work for organizations that employ a number of ex-Forces people in senior positions.

Spend some time reflecting on what you feel are your top three core values and consider asking close friends or family as well. Table 5.1 shows some examples of values to consider. Please use this to help you draw up your shortlist.

Life goals

What do you want from your life? Wow, that's a massive question you may think but people don't spend much time reflecting on what they want from their life.

It is an area that is extremely important to clarify because if you don't have a clear idea of what you want from your life, how are you ever going to achieve it?

Spend some time thinking what it is you truly want from your life longer term – try not to be influenced by others at this point.

Table 5.1

	✔		✔
Loyalty		Happiness	
Integrity		Supportiveness	
Honesty		Passion	
Fun		Security	
Adventure		Endurance	
Variety		Courage	
Trust		Achievement	
Love		Sense of purpose	
Friendship		Curiosity	
Drive		Determination	
Creativity		Caring	
Freedom		Elegance	
Independence		Empathy	
Positivity		Nurturing	
Openness		Intuition	
Wisdom		Enthusiasm	
Honour		Respect	
Authenticity		Other:	
Grace		Other:	
Harmony		Other:	

Yes, your thoughts and ideas will evolve as you progress through your life, but you need some idea at this point in your life otherwise how can you possibly begin down the right path? So begin to put some thought to this.

Where you are right now, what is it you ideally want out of life? Keep asking yourself – what else? Build up a picture in as much detail as you can, draw out your top three life goals and make a note of them under Life goals on Table 5.2.

What I truly want from my life is...

Now go back through all you have learnt from the above life considerations exercises and combine all your thoughts to create a summary of five or six key points to summarize what it is you truly want from your life and include them in the summary chart (Table 5.2).

James's story

James was a Captain in the Army. He had always thrived in his career but had recently begun to question it. This made him feel uncomfortable as he had always been passionate about and loyal to the Army and couldn't understand why he was now questioning it as a career.

He was extremely happy day to day in his job, enjoyed the challenges it gave him... but there was something causing him to question it and he couldn't work out what it was.

During our early coaching sessions we worked on the bigger 'life' picture and it soon became apparent that his values, passions, interests and life plan had changed and were no longer a clear fit with his Army career.

In particular he had a real 'light bulb moment' around the environment. Global environmental issues and challenges had gradually become of real interest and very important to him personally – much more important to him than he actually realized. He had been reading any articles or books on environmental issues he could find, particularly around renewable energies. He was initially quite shocked that this had become of such importance to him.

However, having reflected on it he realized this was the missing link in terms of why he was questioning his Army career and was an area he really wanted to get more actively involved in.

By understanding this, James was able to incorporate this thinking into focusing on career options for him. He realized that the area of renewable energies was indeed of particular interest to him and having researched jobs in that field, it all began to fall into place for him.

James has since signed off from the Army and is currently studying for a diploma in renewable energies. On leaving the Army he plans to work as a project manager in the renewable energies department for one of the big international energy suppliers. His long-term goal is to run his own renewable energy consultancy business.

Final Note

Spend as much time as you can on this area. It may not seem directly relevant to your career but it is crucial in helping you decide on the career direction that is going to be right for you.

Vital pieces of information will emerge from this process which, when combined with the key work considerations, will help you clarify what it is you want from your career.

It will also have a much wider impact in helping you understand what is important to you outside of work and what makes you tick.

Table 5.2

Life considerations	Details
Personality type	1. 2. 3.
Personal interests	1. 2. 3.
Personal strengths	1. 2. 3.
Personal achievements	1. 2. 3.
Core values	1. 2. 3.
Life goals	1. 2. 3.
What I truly want from my life is...	1. 2. 3.

Careers Bank

The Careers Bank exercise is unique and can help you gain clarity around which specific career is going to be right for you if you decide to leave the Armed Forces.

I've used this exercise with Armed Forces leavers ever since I began coaching and it can be extremely effective. It doesn't rely on you cherry picking from a long list of careers that 'may be right for you' – it focuses on your drivers and interests and develops specific career suggestions from there.

Setting up your Careers Bank

The Careers Bank is about capturing an exhaustive list of career ideas in one place. The key is to include ANY career idea you have that is of interest to you, no matter how wild or wacky or boring it may seem to you – if there is some interest, include it in your Careers Bank.

It doesn't matter how much (or little) you know about that particular career at this point; if it sounds of interest, add it to your Careers Bank.

Some people like to write lists of careers ideas they have, some people like to cut out ideas they come across in newspapers, magazines etc. It doesn't matter how you collect your ideas, the key is that you draw them all together in one place – keep a list, folder, diary or keep the cuttings in a drawer. Just make sure you capture them all somewhere so they can be used later on.

Develop your Careers Bank over time (3–4 weeks is a good starting point) and look to develop an exhaustive list of ideas. You are looking for as many ideas as possible – a minimum of 30 would be ideal.

This is a brainstorming process, so consult friends, family etc. Also it's absolutely vital you are open-minded and don't discount any ideas at this stage for any reason – if it sounds of interest, include it.

I have included a blank Careers Bank template (Table 6.1) later in the chapter for you to jot down any thoughts you may have.

How to develop your Careers Bank

Below are some thoughts on how to develop a list of ideas to put into your Careers Bank.

Newspaper jobs section

Open the jobs section of a newspaper and give yourself 10 minutes to quickly skim through the job adverts. Highlight anything which evokes some kind of gut response in you. Don't think about things in too much detail and don't discount things ('…but that job doesn't pay enough, it's in Outer Mongolia' etc) and don't analyse the reasons behind your responses – it doesn't matter at this point.

Tear out all the adverts or parts of adverts you have highlighted and add them to your Careers Bank. It is best to do this with a general jobs supplement so you get plenty of variety.

Web resources

Have a look at some of the large recruitment websites for ideas. The following are some examples of the big recruitment and job directory websites: www.monster.com, www.careerbuilder. com, www.fish4jobs.co.uk/jobs, and www.totaljobs.com.

Books and articles

Read some books on unusual types of careers and guides to the best companies to work for. Below are some examples (see Further Reading):

■ *Offbeat Careers: 60 Ways to Avoid Becoming an Accountant* – Vivien Donald
■ *Dare to be different: 101 Unconventional Careers* – Polly Bird
■ *Odd Jobs: Unusual Ways to Earn a Living* – Simon Kent
■ *Britain's top employers: A guide to the Best Companies to Work for* – Corporate Research Foundation UK.

Personality assessments

A number of online personality assessments give suggested careers for your type at the end of the assessment. As mentioned in Chapter 5, I use www.personalitypage.com with my clients and can recommend it; www.self-directed-search.com is another well-known one. You are asked to pay a small fee for both.

Past dreams and friends' careers

Revisit all those careers you dreamed you might do when you were younger: train driver, firefighter, astronaut, brain surgeon etc. Put a note in your Careers Bank or even visit www.prospects.ac.uk and look up 'Explore types of jobs' to see what those possible careers involve. Add any careers of interest to your Careers Bank.

Also, consider jobs your friends are doing. Do any of them do careers that interest you?

Your career history

Revisit the jobs you've done so far. What did you enjoy about those jobs? What careers incorporate the aspects of your past jobs that you did enjoy?

It's easy to look at the bits of the jobs you didn't enjoy, but what did you enjoy about your past jobs? What else?

Look at your interests

Do you have an interest you could translate into a career? Consider the three interests you came up with under 'Personal interests' for the 'Life considerations' exercise.

Day to day

Keep a lookout. Every day keep looking at the jobs that people have – from colleagues to friends and family, to people you walk past in the street. What are they doing and does it interest you? Sit down and brainstorm with friends and/or family – what work do they think you would enjoy? Capture everything and add it to your Careers Bank. Some people like to carry around a small notebook to add their thoughts to or add them to your PDA etc.

Table 6.1

Career ideas	Career ideas

How to analyse your Careers Bank

Now you should have an exhaustive list of career ideas – as mentioned before, a minimum of 30 ideas would be ideal.

Table 6.2 is an example of a recent client's Careers Bank:

Table 6.2

Career ideas	Career ideas
Pilot	Politician
Carpenter	Charter yacht captain
Explorer	Sailing instructor
Outdoor events organizer	Antique researcher
Travel writer	Wildlife photographer
Journalist	Foreign correspondent
Diplomat	Ambassador
Archaeologist	Expedition organizer
Country park ranger	Yacht broker
Farmer	Antique dealer
Teacher	Harbour master
University lecturer	Yacht designer
Graphic designer	Defence industry manager
Oceanographer	Vet
Architect	Foreign office employee
Lawyer	Historic car restorer

Step 1

You now need to consider what the underlying attraction is for each of your career ideas. What's the key thing that attracted you to each of them? Write a comprehensive list in Table 6.3.

Table 6.3

Career idea	Attraction	Career idea	Attraction

Table 6.4 shows some examples of underlying attractions for this particular client.

Table 6.4

Career ideas	Attraction
Pilot	Travel
Carpenter	Outdoors
Explorer	Travel
Outdoor events organizer	Outdoors
Travel writer	Travel
Journalist	Making a difference
Diplomat	Making a difference
Archaeologist	Variety
Country park ranger	Outdoors
Farmer	Outdoors
Teacher	Making a difference
University lecturer	Making a difference
Graphic designer	Variety
Oceanographer	Outdoors
Architect	Variety
Lawyer	Making a difference
Politician	Making a difference
Vet	Making a difference
Sailing instructor	Outdoors

Step 2

Once you have completed your list you will find there are some common attractions that come out of your list. For this particular client it is easy to see the common attractions – outdoors, travel, making a difference and variety.

Using Table 6.5, write a complete list of your common attractions.

Table 6.5

Common attractions
1.
2.
3.
4.
5.
6.
7.
8.
9.
10.

Now narrow your list down to your top three – the three that you feel are most important to you in your career – and include them in Table 6.6.

Table 6.6

Top three attractions
1.
2.
3.

For the client's example above, the three attractions that came out the strongest were 'Outdoors', 'Making a difference' and 'Variety'.

Step 3

Once you have your top three attractions, consider if each of the attractions were alive in your life, what would you absolutely love to do? Come up with your ideal career for each of the three attractions or combine them into one or two ideal careers if you feel they overlap. This is what you would IDEALLY love to do – don't let reality kick in just yet. Use Table 6.7 to record your findings.

Table 6.7

Attraction	Ideal career
1.	1.
2.	2.
3.	3.

If you are struggling to analyse your Careers Bank, get someone who knows you well to work through the exercise with you.

If you are still struggling, a qualified Career Coach will be able to help you. Please see Chapter 20 on Career Coaching for more information on how to find the right Coach for you.

Step 4

Once you have your top three career ideas, you now need to narrow them down to the one career that is going to be right for you. Often when I get to this stage with my clients they know which one they are going to choose.

The example client I've used combined all three of his attractions to come up with his ideal career of being a United Nations Project Manager – travelling to various countries that were struggling with war, famine etc and helping to instigate solutions on behalf of the United Nations.

For him it ticked all the 'Making a difference' boxes, by helping the various countries and parts of the world struggling with various hardships. 'Variety' would come with the fact that he would be working on a variety of different projects. 'Outdoors' would come with the fact that he wouldn't be bound to one office and would be out and about.

He is now looking at the joining criteria for the United Nations, considering what (if any) additional skills and experiences he needs to gain, networking with various ex-Forces people who work for the United Nations and tailoring his CV so he can apply for this type of role.

One way to check you have chosen the right career is to check back against the information you gathered in Chapters 4 and 5 on work and life considerations. Use Table 6.8 to score your chosen career on a scale of 1–5 against each of the key criteria, 1 being not a great fit, 5 being a perfect fit.

If you score 4 or 5 for each section you are more than likely on the right lines. If not, consider the areas where you scored 3 or under and reflect on other options. Pay particular attention to the scores for what it is you want from your work and life – these should certainly be 4 or 5.

In this example my client scored his chosen career 56 out of 60 and had no doubts it was the right career for him!

The next stage is to develop a realistic action plan and we will consider that in Part 3 of the book. However, at this point it would be good to check on your intention to actually make the changes.

Table 6.8

Career:	
Key working considerations	Score (1–5)
Ideal working environment	
Work motivators	
Favourite work skills	
Professional strengths	
Ideal working day	
What I want from my career	
	Total: /30
Key life considerations	
Personality type	
Personal interests	
Personal strengths	
Core values	
Life goals	
What I want from my life	
	Total: /30
Grand total	/60

Step 5

Using Table 6.9, ask yourself on a scale of 1–10 (1 being no real intention, 10 being completely intend to), how strong is your intention to make the changes? How high is your enthusiasm, and how committed are you – each on a scale of 1–10 – to making these changes?

Table 6.9

Chosen career	Scale 1–10
Level of Intention	
Level of Enthusiasm	
Level of Commitment	

If you score 7 or more, research has shown that you are more than likely to achieve it. If you score less than 7 on any of these, you need to consider why and what you could do to improve it.

The 'reality handbrake'

Up to this point we've been focusing on your 'ideal' career. With a lot of clients the chosen ideal career is a real 'light bulb' moment, the point in time where they finally realize what it is they want to do. The fog lifts, everything falls into place, it 'makes sense' and they become extremely determined and energized to achieve their dream career.

However, for some they don't feel it is a realistic or practical option. They may have scored lowly on the above exercise because they have a genuine reason to resist making the changes.

You may feel you fall into this category – if you do, is it a realistic obstacle that is stopping you from considering this career or an obstacle you are deliberately putting in your way that you can overcome? I would suggest you read Chapter 8, 'Challenges you may face', before you make a definite decision, as it could give you some useful insights. People do block change for a number of different reasons so please think long and hard about it before you give up on your ideal career.

If you still feel it isn't a practical solution for you, don't worry. All the time, energy and work you've put in to this point isn't wasted. You have taken a significant step forward. You now know what your ideal career is and you've got a career direction to aim for.

If there is a practical reason why you can't achieve your dream, you need to revisit your work and life considerations and look at the aspects of your ideal career that would be practical for you. Next consider other career ideas along similar lines to your ideal career.

A good way to explain what I mean is to give you an example.

I had a client not so long ago who had a real passion for animals and, growing up, had always wanted to be a Vet. However, for one reason or another he never got the grades he needed so had discounted it at an early age.

His Careers Bank was full of ideas around animals and his final ideal career was still about being a Vet. Great he said, but the reality of it was that he felt it wasn't practical for him to go back to studying for the years needed to get the grades to become a Vet.

So we considered other options around his obvious passion of working with animals. What could he do that ticked all the right boxes in terms of his ideal career?

By having clarity around the key criteria for him we worked out he wanted to help make animals better. He had a love of horses and in particular racehorses.

We contacted some racing stables and looked at what types of people were responsible for getting horses better other than vets. Well, they said, horses have a lot of back problems and the stables used an osteopath that specialized in treating horses… and that was it, his 'light bulb' moment.

He had never heard of an osteopath specializing in racehorses but he just knew then that that was what he wanted to do. Although the training would still be considerable, it ticked all the right boxes for him.

He is now a qualified osteopath, living and working in Ireland treating racehorses… and absolutely loves it.

Final Note

If you work hard on developing and analysing your Careers Bank it really can help you gain clarity in terms of the direction your career should go in.

Stick within the realms of idealism as long as you can and don't let reality kick in until the end of the exercise. It's key to do that so you don't discount career ideas that could lead you down your ideal career path.

There is one caveat I would like to include at this point and I include it with great caution.

Sometimes (I've come across it twice in five years and neither were Forces leavers) people really struggle to come up with ideas for their Careers Bank – they are lacking energy, positivity, drive, determination and creativity – they completely hit a brick wall with this exercise. No matter how hard they try, they struggle to come up with more than a few loose ideas.

The reason for this in both the instances I have come across was that they were suffering from depression. Once this realization was there, we stopped the coaching; they both received professional help and returned to the coaching afterwards to great effect.

If you think you may be suffering from depression or other mental health issues I would advise you to consult a professional in the first instance. Please see the Appendix for some useful contact details.

'The clearer your vision of what you seek, the closer you are to finding it.'

Richard Bolles (1970)

Part 3

Making a successful transition out of the Armed Forces

Considerations when changing career

So you've decided what career you want to do, but how do you change career successfully and what challenges may you face? Below are some key considerations when looking to make a change.

New occupation, new industry

It is far easier to change occupation and remain in the same industry (eg you may stay in the Army but change from leading an infantry platoon to training recruits) or change industry and remain in the same occupation (eg you may want to remain an aeronautical engineer and switch from the Air Force to working for a civilian airline) than it is to change occupation and industry at the same time.

Consider this when you are looking to change your career but do not give up hope if you decide to change both at once – it is possible, just often more difficult to do so. See Paul's story later in the chapter as an example.

Existing skills and experience

What relevant skills and experiences do you have? How transferable are they to a role outside of the military? How can you add to these skills?

Wherever possible find job descriptions for the type of job you are interested in and look at the key skills and experience requirements – what are the skills and experience gaps you have if any?

Tailor your CV and covering letter accordingly and get professional help on writing an effective CV if necessary. I will go into this in more detail in the relevant chapters, but putting together a strong CV is particularly important to Armed Forces leavers where the skills, achievements and experience aren't necessarily as easily recognizable to non-military people.

Research

Build up your knowledge of the industry you are going to move into – in-depth research into the industry is important. Who are the key players? What makes them so successful? Who are the specialist recruitment consultants? Where are jobs advertised? What are the key magazines targeted at this particular industry? What are the unusual ways people get into the industry? How can you apply this knowledge to your own approach? What training might you need to do?

This is particularly important if you have always worked in the military and have no work experience outside of it. Make good use of the contacts you and the military have in the industry you are considering. There are a lot of official and unofficial networking clubs from breakfast and dinner clubs to commercial networking meetings that you could tap into – see the networking section later in the chapter for more details.

Also make good use of the magazines targeted at Forces leavers – please see the Appendix for examples of the on- and offline press titles available.

Informational interviewing

First introduced by Richard Bolles and further highlighted by John Lees (see the Further reading section in the Appendix), they come under the research umbrella but are potentially such an important tool when considering a career change I wanted to give them a section of their own.

In essence they are research interviews with people in the industry you are looking to move into and they can be extremely effective if approached in the right way.

At the outset you need to tap into your initial network of contacts (including military contacts) and friends you know, and find someone (or a number of people) who works in the industry you want to move into.

You then contact that person (or people) and ask them for an insight into the industry. People are often happy to discuss their work as they have a real interest in it but clam up tight if you ask them for a job!

In particular, if they are ex-military themselves they are often extremely happy to talk to military people and help wherever they can; by getting insight into the industry, you are finding out relevant information to help you in your job search.

Approach

I mentioned a number of questions to consider under the research section earlier in the chapter, but key questions to ask could include such things as: Where do they see the industry in five years' time? How did they get into the industry? How do military people normally get into the industry? Which ex-military people work in the industry? Who are the leading companies in the industry? What do they enjoy about the industry? What is/are the relevant trade press to read, websites to look at, events and exhibitions to go to etc, etc. Always keep the calls or meetings short and concise.

I've found by approaching people this way, they are willing to offer advice and contacts. I've also known people at the end of these calls/meetings to be asked in for an interview for a position they have coming up.

The key to the process is at the end of the call/meeting to ask them for three other contacts in the industry they wouldn't mind you talking to. By repeating this process with each call/meeting you can develop a very good understanding of the industry and some very good contacts, very quickly.

The process takes some planning and thinking through but I know it can work as a number of my Forces clients have used it successfully. In fact I've got a current client called Chris who is a very good example of this.

Chris's story

Chris is an ex-US Air Force pilot. He had an extremely successful career in the Air Force flying fast jets, before moving into a liaison role in the Pentagon.

He recently left the Air Force, moved to the UK and has been looking for a position in a property company in London. At the time of writing this book the UK economy is now officially in recession and the property sector is being hit very hard.

Chris has limited experience in the property sector, limited contacts in the UK and combined with the state of the current UK economy, you would think he is facing a real uphill battle to get a job in property.

However, I am delighted to say that Chris has recently accepted a senior role in a well respected international property company. He achieved this by working extremely hard at developing his network of contacts in London and managed to get a lot of informational interviews with senior people in organizations.

It was as a result of an informational interview that he ultimately received the job offer at the property company.

Networking

I wanted to use this example to highlight the positive effect that networking can have on the job hunt process. Chris, although very bright and articulate, had limited experience in a sector that is being hit extremely hard by the current economic climate, yet managed to achieve his goal of being offered and accepting a job in a very well respected company.

Networking really can have that much of an impact on the job hunt process. (Please see the books by Richard Bolles and John Lees (Further reading) for more details on how to structure an informational interview and pose the right questions.)

Build your network

Build up a list of contacts in the industry you are looking to move into. As your network grows keep a good record of your contacts (a cross-referencing database can be extremely beneficial). Don't be afraid to network – it doesn't need to be the hard sell we often associate with networking. Talk to friends of friends who are in the industry, family friends etc.

This is an area where being in the Armed Forces can often give you a good head start. Use the official and unofficial Forces networks to help you gain contacts in your chosen industry.

In the UK, for example, there are a number of official and unofficial networking opportunities. One such unofficial networking group is Castaways which is a Royal Navy dining club. A lot of these unofficial groups are very select in their membership and don't like to advertise themselves, but they are there and can be a very useful resource, so ask around.

Networking groups and websites

In terms of official Forces networking groups in the UK, 'The List' (www.thelistuk.com) is probably one of the most well known. It offers the opportunity for Forces leavers to network face to face with companies and recruiters who may be interested in recruiting Armed Forces leavers. There are also a number of Regimental Networks in the UK such as Gunners in Business and The Duke of Wellington's London Networking Group that would be worth considering if relevant to your Regiment.

Forces Reunited (www.forcesreunited.org.uk) is a well known site for UK Armed Forces leavers and currently has over 400,000 members.

As well as networking groups targeted at Forces leavers specifically, there are also networking groups that are open to a wide range of professions that may be useful. BNI International (www.bni.com) is one of the most well known and position themselves as the largest business networking organization in the world.

Professional networking sites such as Linkedin (www.linkedin.com) and Plaxo (www.plaxo.com) could be very useful and involve a lot of people looking to network around business opportunities. Even networking sites that focus on the social side of things such as Facebook (www.facebook.com) abd MySpace (www.myspace.com) could be useful in developing networks and potentially useful contacts.

Tips on technique

The key with networking groups is to consider the types of people and professions you want to network with and see if these types of people are involved in the network – if not, then it is likely to be a waste of your time.

Also, contacting the professional association or authority of your target market can be a good way of networking with the relevant people. For example, if you want to work within the Security industry in the UK, the Security Industry Authority (www.the-sia.org.uk) could be a useful organization to contact.

The Appendix contains several lists of websites for networking groups and organizations that may be useful, and I have also included a list of industries that are popular with Forces leavers, as well as a list of companies within those industries which historically are Forces-friendly.

The hidden job market

One area that is often talked about by recruiters and career change specialists is the 'hidden job market'.

A vast majority of jobs are not advertised: newly created jobs, unadvertised positions and most jobs with small, energetic companies. This is the hidden job market, and it makes up a large proportion of potential job opportunities for you. Networking can be a very effective means of opening yourself up to these opportunities.

Gaining work experience

It is so important to gain experience in your chosen career – any type of work experience whether freelance, unpaid work experience, part-time etc would be extremely beneficial.

This is so important to ensure you have chosen the right career path and is particularly important if you have no experience whatsoever outside of the Armed Forces.

Work experience will obviously give you some relevant experience you can then put on your CV which in turn may help you get a job, and it will give you relevant contacts and the opportunity to network. It will also show you whether the reality is the same as your perceived view and should help you get clarity on what you need to do to get a job in that industry; and, if it is the right career for you it should boost your motivation, confidence and determination to make the changes.

You would be amazed by the number of people who make huge career changes without first trying out the work. I think a lot of people avoid trying their potential new career because of the fear it may not be all they had hoped for. It may have been a long and painful journey to get to this point and they want to cling on to their new-found career... surely that's all the more reason to try it rather than going through all the stress and worry of having to change career yet again!

So please, do get some work experience even if it's a day shadowing someone currently doing that type of work, it will give you some insight into what it will really be like and what you need to do to get a job there.

Comprehensive career change strategy

In order to be successful in changing career you need to develop a comprehensive strategy covering all key areas.

Below is a breakdown of the methods used to attract job applicants in the UK. This will vary from industry to industry and country to country but it will give you an indication of the key areas to consider when developing your career change strategy.

Methods used by companies to attract applicants (per cent):

- own website – 75 per cent;
- recruitment agencies – 73 per cent;
- employee referral – 47 per cent;
- speculative application/word of mouth – 44 per cent;
- national newspaper adverts – 42 per cent;
- apprentices/work placements/secondments – 33 per cent.

(UK CIPD Annual Survey Report 2007)

The main reason for highlighting this is to show that a job search strategy should include a number of different approaches including working with recruitment consultants, replying to job adverts, direct applications, networking etc.

I've come across too many people who place too much reliance on one or two of these – normally on recruitment consultants and internet job searches. By utilizing a comprehensive strategy you will speed up the job-hunting process and open yourself up to a number of potential opportunities that wouldn't be available to you otherwise.

Effective use of resources available to you

The Armed Forces around the world offer various resources to their Forces leavers, and the size and nature of the programmes vary from country to country. For example, in the United States the official supporting body is the Transition Assistance Programme (TAP) and in the UK it is The Career Transition Partnership (CTP).

CTP is run by Right Management in conjunction with the Ministry of Defence and offers various courses and resources to UK Armed Forces leavers (dependent on rank and length of service) from help with career direction to putting together an effective CV and action plan.

Please contact the relevant people to work out what support is going to be available to you. For more information on what resources are available to Forces leavers in different countries, please see the Appendix at the end of the book.

Action plans and goal-setting

Making the transition into a new career can be extremely challenging and you need to be realistic and plan effectively in order to make as smooth a transition as possible. Developing a realistic action plan and goal-setting are extremely important parts of making a smooth transition.

You also need to commit your action plan to paper. It is very important to do this as it is a proven fact that you are then far more likely to follow it through.

The first step is to develop SMART goals:

Specific

Measurable

Attainable

Realistic

Timescale

Commit your goals to paper and consider all the obstacles you will need to overcome.

Next chunk your goals down into categories: short (0–6 months); medium (6 months–2 yrs); long term (2+ yrs). This will make it less daunting.

Goal-setting and developing a detailed and realistic action plan takes time and people will often resist doing this as it can feel quite a painful process. However, once completed in the right way it will be of real benefit and is vital in making a successful transition, so make a real effort to do it.

Also don't forget to consider goals outside of your work in order to get a balanced life – we often spend little time considering and reflecting on what we want to achieve outside of work which seems ironic considering we want to enjoy our lives!

Include in your action plan rewards for achieving key milestones – they don't have to be big expensive rewards, just something that makes you feel good for what you've achieved.

I've included an action plan template (Table 7.1) for you to consider, as well as an example action plan (Table 7.2).

Once you've written your action plan do a final check before you begin. Ask yourself, 'Once I've achieved the goals I've set myself, what will I have achieved?'

'A goal is a dream with a date'

(Smith, *What Matters* Most, 2000)

Action plan: example

Table 7.2 is an example of an initial action plan for a Flight Lieutenant in the Royal Air Force who I recently worked with. He wanted to move across to work for an African-based charity, ideally as an Operations Manager.

This was the first plan he put together and hopefully it will give you an insight into the type of things you will need to include in your action plan.

Off the back of this and once the research had been done, he was able to put together a much more detailed plan to work from including goals outside of work and rewards for goals achieved.

Table 7.1

Objective: What I need to achieve	Where am I with this objective now? (Scale 1–10, 10 being completely achieved it)	Action I need to take	How will I know I've been successful?	Possible obstacles	Resources I will need	Review dates	Completion date

Table 7.2

Objective: What I need to achieve	Where am I with this objective now? (Scale 1–10, 10 being completely achieved it)	Action I need to take	How will I know I've been successful?	Possible obstacles	Resources I will need	Review dates	Completion date
Getting to know the industry	2 – done some initial reading as this is a passion of mine	Read books, articles, trade titles, go to events and exhibitions, network etc	Get more confident with the knowledge I have and build up a network of contacts	Time I can allocate is limited	Time	2 weeks	1 month
Help my family understand why I want to change career	1 – not talked to them yet	Explain to them the reasons why I want to change career	When they understand and support me	Misunder-standing	Need to have done some initial research		1 month
Financial stability during transition	1 – don't know what money I will need	Once I've done my research, put together a realistic budget	When I have a realistic budget	Unknown how long it will take to make the transition	Advice from a financial adviser		1 month

Table 7.2 *continued*

Objective: What I need to achieve	Where am I with this objective now? (Scale 1–10, 10 being completely achieved it)	Action I need to take	How will I know I've been successful?	Possible obstacles	Resources I will need	Review dates	Completion date
Practical experience	1 – just starting out	Contact my network to look for work experience and write a targeted CV	Having some work experience under my belt	Lack of relevant contacts and time to put a good CV together	Net-working and advice on putting together a strong CV	2 months	3 months
Get the right full-time role	1 – just starting out	Network with the contacts I have, develop a job search strategy	Get offered the right job	No initial relevant contacts	Use my network effectively	3 months	6 months

Paul's story

Paul had already left the Army when I first met him. He had left a year before and had been struggling to find a long-term career. He had done some contract work in various industries but hadn't settled into any type of role and felt really lost.

Through the coaching process he came to realize that he wanted to work in management consultancy, but how could he make the transition into that particular sector? He had little relevant experience, knew very little about the industry and had no contacts whatsoever.

The answer was to develop a comprehensive job-search strategy combining very good research, networking and planning.

Paul was four weeks into his job search when I spoke to him, and he then had second interviews with four top consultancies, and not one of the roles he was being considered for was being advertised… this is the hidden job market. I was sure it wouldn't be long before Paul got the break he thoroughly deserved.

Paul will not only have moved industries but also occupation – in one career move. So it is possible!

Final Note

Research before job search – make sure you research thoroughly. With the advent of the internet you have no excuses.

Then develop a comprehensive career change strategy as well as a clear and realistic action plan and put them into action!

And finally, pick up the phone... don't leave it until tomorrow; and don't be afraid to use your network and contact new people – if you do it the right way, it will open up new opportunities and ultimately pay dividends for you.

'Find a job you like and you add five days to every week.'

H Jackson Brown Jr

8

Challenges you may face

So you want to leave the Armed Forces, but what are the challenges you may face? Below are some examples.

Financial

People often feel the biggest barrier to change is money... I can't afford it... I'm never going to be able to make enough money from that... I'm not going to be able to afford the mortgage... I've got a family to support etc.

Financial worries can be such a destroyer of dreams. All salaries being equal, would you do your current job or something else?

If you knew that your new career was definitely going to be the right choice for you, that you were going to be extremely happy, successful and really enjoy it, would your financial concerns stop you from making the change?

I always remember a passage in the book Voyage by the 1960's movie star Sterling Hayden.

> To be truly challenging, a voyage, like a life, must rest on a firm foundation of financial unrest... 'I've always wanted to sail to the south seas, but I can't afford it.' What these men can't afford is not to go. They are enmeshed in the cancerous discipline of security. And in the worship of security we fling our lives beneath the wheels of routine. And before we know it our lives are gone.
>
> What does a person need, really need? A few pounds of food each day, heat and shelter, six feet to lie down in – and some form of working activity that will yield a sense of accomplishment. That's all, in the material sense, and we know it. But we are brainwashed by our economic system until we end up in a tomb beneath a pyramid of time payments, mortgages, preposterous gadgetry, playthings that divert our attention from the sheer idiocy of the charade.
>
> The years thunder by. The dreams of youth grow dim where they lie caked in dust on the shelves of patience. Before we know it, the tomb is sealed.
>
> Where, then, lies the answer? In choice. Which shall it be: bankruptcy of purse or bankruptcy of life?
>
> Sterling Hayden (1999, pp84–5)

An extreme view maybe, but he certainly had some valid points.

There are many pressures on us financially and it can be difficult to see past them. Often the better paid the job, the more pressure and the longer the hours you will work (of course there are exceptions to this!).

What is the right balance for you between pay and the time you are willing to commit to work?

As I mentioned before, a strong belief I hold is that if you find what it is you are truly going to enjoy, you will apply yourself and be motivated – as a result you are likely to be a success... with success, money often follows.

One practical aspect that could help is careful financial planning to cover the period of transition. You could take a mortgage holiday, dip into savings etc. Please talk to a financial adviser about your options.

Emotional challenges

You may have looked at the heading of this section and thought that it doesn't apply to you. You may think that due to the extremely stressful situations you've been under in combat etc and the training you've had, you won't have any emotional challenges in transitioning out of the Forces.

My experiences with Forces leavers shows you could well be wrong because it can be a real challenge no matter what experiences and training you've had, so please read on.

Whenever I finish working with a Forces leaver they will have a clear idea of what career they want to do and a detailed timing plan of how to get there. They are relieved, excited, energized, motivated, committed, resourceful etc... and yet some of them never go on to make the changes. What stops them?

Fear and negativity

There are a number of contributing factors, but one of the key things that often stops them is fear – fear that they won't succeed in their new career, that they're not bright enough, that they've not got enough money, that their family will be much happier staying where they are, that they don't have the right qualifications etc.

For Forces leavers, it can be the fear of leaving the protective umbrella of the Armed Forces that can be one of the biggest challenges. Even the most ardent and committed person can come to a grinding halt.

This negative self-talk that we all have, or 'gremlins' as they are often called, stop a lot of people from achieving their full potential.

According to Michael Voight, PhD, a sports psychologist at the University of Southern California, 'Of the 66,000 thoughts we typically have per day, 70 to 80 per cent are negative.'

A depressing statistic maybe, but it shows the level of internal turmoil people can experience. Imagine the impact this can have on making big decisions in your life such as deciding to leave the Armed Forces!

You've already done much more than the average person who is unhappy with their job just by reading this book (most people spend more time planning their holidays than their careers!); don't come to a grinding halt now.

Yes, some of your fears may be legitimate, but by being aware of your gremlins and working to minimize your negative self-talk, you are in a much stronger position to understand what are legitimate concerns and obstacles and what are challenges you can overcome.

I am not a gremlin guru, nor do I attain to be. I do, however, understand the impact both positive and negative mindsets can have... I have seen it first hand in enough of my clients.

There are a number of good books on this subject (see the Self-esteem/Self-confidence section in the Further reading section) and some great techniques to help work with your gremlins which are covered in these books.

> Our doubts are traitors, and make us lose the good we oft might win, by fearing to attempt.'
>
> William Shakespeare (1604–5)

Dave's story

At the time of writing I had a current client who was struggling to come to terms with his gremlins around change.

Dave knew exactly what career he wanted to move into but every time he had looked to leave the Navy in the past he had never gone through with it. The reason he gave me was 'it never felt right'.

He had been in the Navy for a number of years and, although he had a lot of great experiences, he was completely miserable and very down about it.

It transpired it was his gremlins stopping him from making the changes he so wanted to make. Looking back over his life there was a pattern of this happening over and over again.

His gremlins kept saying 'STOP! You are much better off where you are... don't risk it because things will only get worse if you do.'

Every time he considered a change his gremlins blocked him. It was only by asking him what was really stopping him, and seeing the same pattern throughout his life, that he realized it was his gremlins.

Initially, by realizing this, it changed his whole outlook and relieved some of the pressure he had put himself under. He then started to understand his particular gremlins and felt he could finally start to move on with his career. The proof is in the pudding of course and we still need to finish the coaching, but his mindset does seem to have changed considerably with this realization.

Influencers

Other influencers on how we think or feel are family, friends and influential figures. They often have a huge impact on what we think and believe – whether consciously or subconsciously. Although they think they have your best interests at heart, they provide their own personal views which may not always be the right ones for you.

It is extremely important to make up your own mind. Ultimately you are the only one who knows what is going to be right for you. Don't get me wrong, consider the advice they give, just bear in mind it is based on their own views and beliefs and not yours.

Success

Society has a lot to blame around the pressures we often put ourselves under. If you said someone was successful with their career, what are you basing 'success' on? For a lot of people a big proportion is based on the fact that they are earning a lot of money and have all the trappings and status that goes with that.

Success = loads of money!

I would question that. Yes, money will often follow if someone is particularly successful at something, but not always. We as a society put too much pressure and emphasis on salary levels determining if someone is very 'successful' at their job.

Look at people who work in the financial markets – someone might be pretty average at their job and still earn what we might consider to be a huge amount of money. Does that mean they are successful?

Money is an article which may be used as a universal passport to every-where except heaven, and as a universal provider for everything except happiness.

Wall Street Journal

Success is a feeling. It's about how you feel inside; it's not about how others view you. They can't make you feel successful!

Risk

Also, how do you perceive risk? How much of a risk are you willing to take to find the right career for you? If you perceive the risk as being too great you won't make the changes you want, so what can you do to reduce the risk?

Understand you may need to take 'risks' to succeed. I'm not talking about uncalculated risks; I'm talking about calculated, thought-through risks – you've only got one life and limited time on this planet, so make the most of it. Step out of your comfort zone – that's often what's needed to make the necessary changes.

What are you willing to sacrifice to be 'successful'? Generally the more money you are paid, the more responsibility you will have, the greater the pressures, the longer the working hours, less time at home etc.

Sarah's story

Sarah was a Corporal in the Army. Although she had been successful in her Army career to date she was now extremely unhappy. It felt unfulfilling; she had no sense of satisfaction or belief in what she was doing.

She would spend her time off dreading the thought of having to go back to work and really wasn't herself anymore. She used to be really active outside of work, happy and upbeat – now she just felt low and lacked energy.

Sarah knew what career she wanted to move into but it took her nearly two years to move on. Why?

Two main reasons: the fear of the unknown, and worrying that she wasn't going to be able to make enough money to pay her mortgage and be able to afford to live.

Eventually she suffered from a bout of depression and in her words 'shut down'. She lost energy, enthusiasm, motivation and came to a grinding halt.

After a period of counselling she came out of the depression, her enthusiasm and energy returned. She decided that was the final straw and that she was going to make changes in her life.

Originally from New Zealand, Sarah was an amateur artist who drew on New Zealand's Maori heritage as inspiration for her paintings. She had always wanted to try her hand at being a professional artist but had never had the courage to make the change... until recently.

She now lives in London and works as a professional artist. When I last spoke to her she had just had her first two exhibitions and her Maori-inspired paintings were selling extremely well. She hasn't looked back.

Skills shortage

There are now more and more flexible ways of learning new skills and provided you are realistic in the transition you are looking to make and have a detailed action plan including the skills you need to learn, there is often no reason you can't fill your skills gaps, especially with the support and courses available to Forces leavers.

The potential 'easier option'

There are certain industries that Forces leavers are often drawn to and where it is potentially easier to find work than in other industries – for example, working in the defence or security industries.

If working in one of these industries is what you would ideally love to do, then great, go for it. However, if it isn't your ideal career and you are considering it because it is going to be potentially easier for you to get a job there than in your ideal industry, then resist doing it.

The reason for this is that in the long term it is unlikely to make you happy and you will be back in the same position as you are now, having to go through the process of changing career yet again.

If, for example, you are using it as a stepping stone to build up skills gaps etc and it is going to take you on the right path to achieving your ideal career, then great.

Time

Time is precious to us all and you will need to allow a significant amount of time for making a successful career transition – more than you will probably initially think.

As we mentioned earlier, Forces leavers are in the unique position that you may have months, even years after having signed off before you can start your new job, so make sure you make the most of the time available and do not leave your planning until the last minute.

This has a real advantage in terms of planning the transition, plugging skills gaps etc. The flip side is that a lot of companies won't recruit until you are from, say, between one to three months from becoming available to start that job. This creates a real catch 22: you don't want to sign off before you have a job to go to but you may not be able to get agreement on a job offer until you have signed off and are near to leaving.

Also with two major conflicts in Iraq and Afghanistan, a number of Armed Forces are being stretched, meaning longer and more frequent tours to the war zones and less time at home.

You need to utilize the time you do have as effectively as possible, develop a realistic action plan, and deliver on it.

Final Note

It is often the emotional barriers which stop us from making the changes that are so needed... we often know in our heart of hearts that a change is needed, but the emotional barriers stop us from making the right decisions.

Some say it is a matter of balance – the positive and negative things in our lives balance themselves out and it is only when there is imbalance one way or the other that you actually make changes... I would hope that we could choose to re-address the balance when we wanted to.

Far better is it to dare mighty things, to win glorious triumphs, even though checkered by failure, than to take rank with those poor spirits who neither enjoy much nor suffer much, because they live in the grey twilight that knows not victory nor defeat.

Theodore Roosevelt

9

Qualities you will need

A lot of books and career advisers focus on helping people find the right career but not many focus on helping them through the transition itself.

When I first started coaching I thought by far the hardest part would be in helping people work out what was going to be the right career for them. Now, with experience, I know that ensuring people are actually making the transition is equally as difficult if not more difficult for some.

So what can be done to ensure that you do make the desired transition? Different things are going to work for different people, but initially you need some key qualities – self-awareness, self-belief, self-confidence, courage, determination and positivity.

Self-awareness

To find your true passion you need to have a good understanding of yourself – in other words good self-awareness. I have found those with good self-awareness are often purposeful, motivated, energetic and successful. Spend time on getting to know yourself better.

If you felt your self-awareness was low before you started to read this book, hopefully you will have begun on the journey of understanding yourself more having gone through the various exercises in the book. I would hope you have more of an understanding of what is important to you and what makes you tick – both at work and outside of work.

Self-belief

I've mentioned in Chapter 8 the impact key people in your life can have on how you think and feel. The process of going through a career transition can feel like a very lonely place full of self-doubt, and having key people in your life helping and supporting you through change can be a big motivating factor and help with your self-belief.

Also, you need to believe the changes are for the best. A question I am commonly asked is 'How do I know I am going to be successful at this?' Well, you don't know for sure but if you've done your research, you've set a realistic action plan and covered all the eventualities you can think of then you've done as much as you can. You will only truly know once you've tried it.

A really important point not to forget is that you will often be quite a long way through your planning before you actually have to make any significant changes. By that time you should be much more knowledgeable and confident that you are making the right decision.

This is something a lot of people forget – they think that

because they have in principle made a decision to leave the Armed Forces that the change is already done... and that can be a scary prospect, because: at that point you probably haven't done the detailed research you need to; you probably haven't got any work experience; you may not have the relevant qualifications yet, etc etc.

It's only at the point where you have collected all the information and knowledge you need that you will begin to feel confident you are making the right decision.

Have you heard of self-fulfilling prophecies? These are when you believe something is going to happen and it actually does end up happening. They can be both positive and negative: if you believe you are going to fail at something, the likelihood is you will fail! Therefore, if you believe you are going to succeed...

Self-confidence and courage

You need self-confidence and courage to take the first step and make the changes happen. This goes hand in hand with self-belief – people who make big career changes don't often see themselves as courageous, it's just something they feel they 'had to do'.

How much do you want a better working life? How much are you not enjoying your current working life? If you knew you were going to be successful at your new career, how much do you think you would enjoy it? If you were retired looking back at this period of your life, what would you advise yourself to do now?

What gives us courage? The thought of a better life, fear of failure, a clear picture of what it is we want etc.

Ill-health and near-death experiences are huge factors that drive people and often give them the courage to make the changes they desire... mostly they wish they had made the changes much much earlier. We all have different drivers; what gives you courage?

What e're thou art, act well thy part. (Inscription, Scottish doorway)

Smith, H (2000)

Determination, determination, determination

You will need determination to follow things through, so never give up! You will potentially come up against some big challenges and obstacles that will need overcoming – you will need to be determined and resilient.

I'm not talking about being obstinate and blinkered. If something isn't working you need to reassess and not keep banging your head against a brick wall – determination is something different.

The analogy below about two kittens rang true with me, and highlights the difference that determination can make.

Two kittens were playing in the farmyard and came across a full pail of cream. They fell into the pail and were in kitty heaven. They drank and drank the cream but then realized that the pail was too deep for them to climb out though they tried and tried. The other kittens in the farm gathered around the top of the pail and when they saw how deep it was they taunted the kittens and told them they were going to drown.

Both kittens ignored the comments and carried on attempting to jump out of the pail. Finally one of the kittens took heed of what the other kittens were saying and gave up, falling to the bottom of the pail and drowning.

The other kitten struggled with intense determination and belief that it could get out of the pail. It struggled so much it turned the cream into butter and was able to climb out. On seeing this all the other kittens were curious. 'Why did you continue to attempt to climb out of the pail when we were tormenting you, saying "you'll never do it."?' Another said 'we were laughing at you, telling you that you were stupid and going to die.' Another asked, 'Why didn't you give up and die like the other kitten?' The kitten paused and said, 'Oh! I'm slightly deaf. You see I thought you were encouraging me to climb out.'

Coaching Manual, UKCLC (2003)

Positivity

The ability to remain positive through the ups and downs that will happen during transition is important.

Being positive can open up all sorts of opportunities. People are often willing to help people with a positive outlook and adversely, to avoid people who are downbeat and negative. Being positive can help to open new doors and for you to consider new opportunities.

The thought of your new career should give you lots of enthusiasm and energy. Read inspiring books, listen to inspiring music, watch inspiring movies, go running regularly, go to the gym – do something that naturally lifts you and makes you positive.

If you don't have a positive attitude in business and in life, you will never, ever be successful.

Donald Trump

Final Note

A number of these qualities interlink and although it is difficult to quantify the effect having these will have on making a smooth career transition, it is certainly my experience that the people with these qualities are going to find a transition much easier.

As a Forces leaver, a number of these qualities are likely to already be ingrained in you (even if you don't think so!), so make good use of them.

10

Rising to the challenge

OK, so how do I develop these qualities and overcome the challenges that lie ahead?

You may be thinking along the lines of… 'At the moment I'm just really worried. It seems such a big step, so daunting, and I just don't know whether I'm going to enjoy civilian life.'

Below are a number of ways to overcome the challenges you may encounter.

What is your target?

Be very clear on what it is you want and take time to think it through.

Ensure you are extremely clear of the career changes you want to make. What will your new career ideally look like? Build up as clear a picture in your mind as you possibly can and write it all down.

A lot of people feel under so much pressure trying to juggle their day to day lives that they don't give themselves time to think this through. Take time out, take a holiday, travel somewhere new, go running or go for a simple walk – do something to get away from the day to day challenges of your life so you feel refreshed and can get an objective view on your life.

I often hear from clients that they get up early, work late, grab a quick bite to eat in front of the TV then it's off to bed to do the same thing again the next day. At weekends or when they have time off work, they are so tired they spend the time recharging, preparing to go back to work!

How much time do you actually allocate to thinking about how things are going and what you want to do moving forwards? Generally the answer is very little to none!

How are you supposed to learn and make changes in your life if you don't allow any time to do this?

> Suppose you were to come upon someone in the woods working feverishly to saw down a tree.
>
> 'What are you doing?' you ask.
>
> 'Can't you see?' comes the impatient reply. 'I'm sawing down this tree.'
>
> 'You look exhausted!' you exclaim. 'How long have you been at it?'
>
> 'Over five hours,' he returns, 'and I'm beat! This is hard work.'
>
> 'Well why don't you take a break for a few minutes and sharpen your saw?' you inquire. 'I'm sure you will go a lot faster.'
>
> 'I don't have time to sharpen the saw,' the man says emphatically. I'm too busy sawing!'
>
> Covey, S (1999)

If you are in a job you have struggled with for a considerable length of time, it is going to start taking its toll. Don't forget we spend so much of our waking hours at work, if you aren't happy then it is going to start having a knock-on effect on the other areas of your life: Sunday night blues; taking your frustrations out on others; lack of energy and motivation to do things outside of work; loss of sex drive; comfort eating; depression etc.

It can be a miserable downward spiral and sometimes the only way to break the cycle is to make significant changes which may involve a job change.

Imagine a different future

Imagine yourself a year down the line working successfully in your new career. What are you doing? Who are you working with? How do you feel?

Once you are doing the thing you love and are passionate about, your energy levels lift massively, you don't feel as if you're battling all day… 'Find the job you love and you'll never have to work another day again.' Corny line and I never used to believe it… but it's true. Yes, we all have bad days every now and again but generally your working days should be fun, positive, full of energy and effortless at times. It can happen; I know because its how I now feel.

Also I've seen that things begin to drop into place for people who are on the right track, chance meetings with the right people, winning pieces of work seemingly effortlessly – it often feels like luck, but there must be something in it as it seems to happen a lot for people who are truly on the right path.

Listen to your intuition

What's going to make you happy? What are you truly going to enjoy? It comes back to the belief around finding your true passion.

Too often people focus on what is going to make them the most money. When I ask people what is going to make them truly happy, they often have no idea because they have spent so much of their time and energy focusing on what is going to make them the most money!

Listen to your instincts and intuition – they often set the alarm bells ringing consciously or unconsciously, but few people really develop the skill of really listening to what their intuition is telling them. Our instincts and intuition are rarely wrong so it's a good skill to develop.

I recently had a client who was looking for a job and she came across an advert in the paper which highlighted all the benefits of a particular job but didn't actually say what it was. She rang up and was told it was for a real estate agency and was persuaded to go to an open day to find out more information.

The 'open day' turned out to be a series of very intense interviews throughout the day. The next day she was called and offered a job and put under considerable pressure to accept there and then and that they wanted her to start the next day. She accepted as she wanted a job and the money was good.

She called me later on in the day to ask my views as she was beginning to have doubts. I asked her what her intuition was telling her – she said it was screaming at her to say no!

Following on from that realization, and having worked through why her intuition might be reacting like that, it became obvious to her that the job really wasn't for her. She called the company back and declined the offer.

Think of yourself!

I'm not talking about being overly selfish, but ultimately you need to find a way of being happy. Sounds obvious I know, but a lot of Forces people resist leaving because of the fear that it will have a negative impact on their family and that their family won't be happy.

Staying in the Forces in this scenario would be fine in the short term but in the long term if you are unhappy, that will have a negative impact on the people closest to you anyway.

Changing career can seem an extremely selfish thing – me, me, me! This can be especially true with leaving the Forces due to the fact that your family may need to relocate, leaving a lot of friends behind etc.

Others often have to make sacrifices for your dreams to come true. Keep talking to those people because they will understand if they believe this is truly what you want to do and what will make you happy.

Trust

Trust in your own abilities and realize that we all have doubts and fears when we make big changes. Everyone going through a career transition will have doubts at some stage or other, no matter how confident they are on the outside – you are not alone.

Learn from your mistakes

Something your parents would say to you, but something very important if you are to progress with your life and not just repeat the same cycle.

If something isn't working, analyse what went wrong and ensure you don't make the same mistake again and move on. We all make mistakes, the successful people are the ones that learn from them and move on.

Make your mistakes work for you by learning from them.

Donald Trump

Don't take life too seriously

I recently heard this from a client who was a fighter pilot in the second Gulf War. It seemed such a strange thing for him to say when he was in such a serious job, but he said it helped him get a perspective on things and cope better with the pressure he was under. Good advice.

Think outside of your career

Sometimes only small changes (or no changes at all!) are needed in the workplace. It could be outside the workplace where the biggest changes are actually needed and that you are looking to make changes in the wrong area.

I once had a client who felt unfulfilled and he thought it was his job causing him to feel like that. It actually transpired that the right solution for him was doing some voluntary work alongside his job. Check – make sure you are looking to make changes in the right area of your life.

Celebrate!

One thing that can make a big difference to your motivation is to celebrate goals as you achieve them.

Some cultures are better than others at this. For example: a big generalization, but Americans are often good at celebrating success whereas the British can be dreadful at this. The British are often quick to move on to the next goal without taking stock and appreciating what they have achieved.

If you achieve a goal, celebrate it. That can be anything from throwing a party or going on a dream holiday, to having a coffee break, a day off to spend with your family – whatever is right for you; but do **something** – it will revitalize you!

Don't give up

Finally, don't give up if you don't make the changes you want to now – keep working at it and reflect on what may be stopping the changes from happening. Don't let your gremlins win, keep planning and moving forwards with your goals.

Once they start down a new path, people often feel some of the pressure coming off. Sometimes they feel a huge burden on them when they have to make a decision on the right career path, as they feel it is such a big decision, 'for the rest of their lives' etc.

The key as mentioned earlier is that you should not be making a big leap into the unknown; you will have researched the market, talked to people in it and have got some sort of work experience before you are even at the point where you need to make a decision. By that point you will be much more knowledgeable, confident and able to make a judged decision.

Final Note

There isn't necessarily a quick fix here. It could take time to overcome your challenges, but by being aware of them and considering ways of overcoming them, I am sure you will succeed.

11

Developing the right approach

You've worked out what is the right career for you, what changes you need to make, what potential challenges are along the way and you've put a detailed and realistic action plan together. Now you need to get into action.

You've broadly got two main routes: self-employment or being employed by others. If you are going to be self-employed, the focus initially should be on putting together a comprehensive business plan as this will draw together all your thoughts at this stage.

Self-employment

Business planning is critical, and should be considered early on in the process of developing a new business. One of the key things a business plan will highlight, if done in a thorough manner, is whether the business idea is a potentially viable proposition. A business plan will:

■ raise key questions you may not have considered;

■ get you to consider your competition;

■ focus on costings – setting up and ongoing; and, as part of the process...

■ develop a detailed action plan.

There are a number of places where you will find business plan templates to work from, but the new-business adviser at your bank would be a good starting point. A lot of banks now offer good interactive CD ROMs to help you put together a comprehensive business plan. Please see the Appendix for some other useful resources to consider.

Employment by an organization

If you are going to be employed by others then you will be going through the job interview process – the chapters that follow will provide tips to help you through the process.

One of the most critical things you need to do as a Forces leaver is to translate your skills, strengths, achievements and experiences into something that non-military personnel will understand. This is a key consideration when making a successful transition, and with Forces acronyms and jargon it can be difficult for non-military people to decipher what you have done and achieved that is relevant. I will talk about this in more detail in Chapter 12 – CV/Résumé considerations.

You also need to become streetwise on the ways of approaching organizations to the best effect – there are effective and not so effective ways of doing this. For example, if you are approaching a large organization, it is unlikely you will get a good response from an e-mail you send to a 'general' company e-mail address such as admin@xxx.com or info@xxx.com.

Obtaining contact details

The key is, you need to work as hard as you can to get the contact details for the relevant person – normally your potential boss. It can sometimes be hard to do this, as companies have a lot of 'gatekeepers' as I call them – people such as secretaries, receptionists and Human Resource personnel who don't want to give out this type of information, and will ask you to e-mail or write to Human Resources or a general company e-mail address.

So how do you get the name and contact details of the person you want to get in touch with? Your own network of contacts may be able to help or you can try a number of different approaches – looking on the website and asking reception would be a good starting point. Look to get the relevant person's name at the very least, because you can probably work out their e-mail address by looking at other people's e-mail addresses in the company on the website, eg lots of companies use firstname.surname@companyname.com.

If you are struggling to even get their name, call the company out of office hours when receptionists have gone home and phonecalls are often picked up by other employees who are more likely to give you the person's name.

One reason why you are looking to get the boss's details is that although they may not actively be looking for someone with your experience and skills, they could be having some initial thoughts on a role you would be perfect for – you are then at the top of their list and they may end up only interviewing you and offering you the job (this is an example of the hidden job market, discussed in Chapter 7). The other reason is that they may be so impressed by you that they create a role specifically for you.

More about technique

As we said earlier, try to avoid sending your details to Human Resources in the first instance as they can act as gatekeepers – if there isn't an active job being advertised in the department you are looking to work in, they will be unlikely to pass on your details.

Also, if you are calling someone at work, try them early or late in the day as people are often more willing to talk at those times – people are often struggling to keep on top of meetings, conference calls, report writing etc during the day – apart from Monday mornings, which are not a good time to call someone generally!

In terms of how you apply, please consider the relevant sections on how to put your CV/résumé and cover letter together (Chapters 12 and 13).

12

CV/Résumé considerations

As mentioned at the beginning of Part 3, a strong CV or résumé is a vital piece of information in your job search and particularly important when looking to leave the Armed Forces, as non-military people can find it difficult to see the transferability of skills and experiences you may have.

Even if you decide to set up your own business, a CV can give you an objective view on your skills and experience and the areas you are going to need to develop.

CV format

Presentation

A big debate over CVs for Forces leavers is how to present the information in the CV to best effect. In the UK there are two main types of CV format: a classic reverse-chronological (most common type), or a skills-based CV – both formats have their advantages and disadvantages.

A reverse-chronological CV shows a clear career path and development but doesn't clearly show the transferability of the skills and relevant experience of a Forces person. The skills-based CV shows the transferability of skills clearly, but not necessarily a clear career path.

A hybrid of the two seems to be a common approach by Forces leavers and the one that seems to be well received by organizations: a reverse-chronological CV, highlighting key relevant skills and achievements at the beginning, before the career history.

I deliberately haven't included any sample CVs as the right CV will vary considerably, not only from country to country but also between different industry sectors. View your CV as a constantly evolving document; get feedback from employers and recruiters wherever possible and keep adapting and tailoring it.

Length

In terms of the length of a CV, the recommended length varies from country to country: in the United States and some of mainland Europe a one-page summary CV is common; in the UK two pages is the norm.

Content

You are also likely to get conflicting advice on what to put in your CV – people have personal preferences on what they like to see in a CV and how they like it formatted, so bear this in mind when you're getting feedback on your CV. Ask yourself when you get feedback if you feel the changes advised will enhance your CV in relation to the roles you are applying for.

Layout and style

When you are looking to put your CV together, recruitment consultants that specialize in placing ex-Forces people should be able to give you some good insights and advice on layout, what to include in your CV and how to include it. Please see Chapter 14, 'Effective use of recruitment consultants', for more information.

Also, the mistake that a lot of Forces leavers make is in the use of jargon and military acronyms in their CVs. Even such things as job titles may not be easily understood by non-military personnel – give a good descriptor or equivalent civilian role if applicable. This is obviously easier with some job titles than others but could help with understanding your level and breadth of experience. If you are unsure of an equivalent civilian role, ask a recruiter – they should be able to help.

What to include in your CV

- Positive, concise factual statements – no waffle!
- Focus on achievements, the difference you made in your roles, and give quantifiable evidence to support this: ££; percentage savings; profits etc. This isn't so important for the US market, but is critical for the UK and other markets.
- Show your relevant skills, qualifications and experience; what are the key skills, qualifications and experiences your potential employer is looking for? Look at the job description for the role, and show the skills/qualifications/experiences you have that match those requirements (or the requirements for a similar role).
- Give your career history and don't leave any gaps.
- Give information about you: personality; motivations; work style; attitude.

- Focus on your most current roles; for your most current/relevant roles, ensure the information is more detailed.
- Make sure your CV is clear and easy to read – consistent font size and style, good use of white space etc.
- Ensure the key points you are looking to get across are on the front page if possible.
- Personalize your CV for each application, focusing on the key relevant points – I know it is time-consuming but it can make a real difference.
- Do not write in the first person.

What NOT to include in your CV

- Don't include any negatives.
- Don't give any opinions or lie on your CV.
- Don't use slang, jargon, joking etc; eg make sure your e-mail address looks/sounds professional.
- Keep non-essential information, eg weight, height etc, to a minimum.
- Don't provide reference details – these can be provided later on.
- Don't give reasons for leaving past jobs – it can always be discussed in interview if brought up.
- Don't give past salaries on your CV – again, it can be discussed in interview if brought up.
- Don't repeat anything.
- Absolutely no typos! Spellcheck it but don't rely on spellcheck software – double-check it yourself.

Final Note

The key with your CV is to convey your experience, skills and achievements in a manner that is easily understood by non-military people.

One of the important things to focus on is transferable skills. Use the results from Table 4.3 on page 26 to help you draw out what your key transferable skills are.

Also, imagine yourself in the shoes of the person who is going to be reading your CV. Often they will have a large pile of CVs to go through and will have a quick scan (less than a minute) of each CV to decide whether it requires further reading is to be discarded. If they feel it has potential it will be put in another pile for further consideration later on.

You obviously want to ensure your CV doesn't go in the bin, so it needs to be concise, clear to read, and for the relevant information to be prominent.

Ultimately the role of your CV is to get you an interview, so don't undersell yourself, but equally, make sure you can back up any claims you make.

13

Effective letter-writing

Traditional cover letters are gradually becoming a thing of the past with the use of e-mail but they do still have their place in the job application process.

If writing to a recruitment consultant it is common practice to e-mail your CV as a Word document (some prefer a PDF document as it keeps the formatting correct) with a brief covering e-mail highlighting the reasons for writing and any particularly relevant experience you may have. Please see Chapter 14, 'Effective use of recruitment consultants', for more details.

How to approach companies direct

If you are applying speculatively to a company for a job and have the relevant person's e-mail address, send an initial e-mail with your CV and cover letter attached, as well as putting a hard copy of your CV and cover letter in the post.

If applying for an advertised job, there is usually an e-mail address to send your CV and cover letter to. Some companies still request hard copies and obviously send a hard copy if requested. Also some companies have their own application forms and processes so a cover letter (and possibly CV) is redundant.

When you apply for a role in a company, whether advertised or speculatively, make a note of when you sent the application. If you haven't heard from them within two to three days after they should have received the application, call the relevant person to check they received it. These phone calls can be very effective if positioned in the right way.

You need to convey the fact that you are purely phoning to check they have received your application. I've found that by positioning the call in this way and not pushing for a meeting, you can open up a positive dialogue. If the person has time they might well pull up your CV whilst you are on the phone and may even make a decision there and then to invite you in for an interview.

As we mentioned earlier in the book, in the Appendix there is a list of industry sectors popular with Forces leavers as well as a list of companies that historically are Forces-friendly, which may be of interest to you.

Content

I haven't included any sample cover letters for the same reasons that I haven't included any sample CVs – in that they will vary so much between the countries and companies that you apply to. I have, however, included some key considerations when putting a cover letter together.

Key considerations

■ Send your letter to the head of department, not the HR department.

■ Limit it to one side of A4.

■ As with your CV, make sure the letter is clear and easy to read – consistent font size and style etc.

■ Keep it concise and avoid starting every sentence with 'I'.

■ Make sure you are clear about what you are applying for.

■ Pull out 2–3 key points from your CV as to why the organization should consider you.

■ Point out why you want to work for that particular organization – research any recent awards they've won, recent client wins, share price etc; it gives a very positive impression.

■ Keep it positive, factual, concise and professional.

■ No typos!

■ Be clear on the next steps you are looking for – if you are looking for a meeting, be clear that that is what you are looking for.

■ As mentioned earlier in the chapter, phone to check the letter has arrived.

Final Note

Cover and speculative letters are often overlooked or little time is spent putting them together, but they are there to get the person to read your CV – without a strong cover letter your CV may not get read.

With a little bit of planning you can put a strong cover or speculative letter together and ensure the potential employer looks in more detail at your CV, which is the ultimate point of the letter.

14

Effective use of recruitment consultants

Recruiters can be very useful when looking to move out of the Armed Forces. There are a number of recruiters who specialize in placing Forces people and they are often ex-Forces people themselves.

Often they will have a good understanding of the Forces, the job market, transferable skills, putting together an impact-making CV, and also of letting you know how realistic your chances are of getting the type of role you are considering, and what you need to do to increase your chances.

Recruiters can also be a good sounding board when looking to consider your monetary value in the commercial world, although also, don't forget to consider salary surveys (current accurate salary predictions for specific roles/industries).

How to approach Recruitment Consultancies

Recruitment consultancies are extremely busy, and are initially unlikely to want to talk to you until they have received your CV. Firstly, I would recommend finding the e-mail address of the relevant consultant and e-mail them your CV in the first instance with a brief cover e-mail highlighting the type of role you are looking for and the key relevant experience you have. Calling reception or looking on the website should find you the relevant person's e-mail address.

I would then follow up the e-mail the next day with a quick phone call to ensure they received your CV and to ideally arrange to meet them.

It is normal to be invited for a meeting face to face with a recruiter, but if time is pressing and they have a role they would like to put you forward for – and the deadline for applications is imminent – they may request a phone interview.

Use of information

One thing to consider when talking to recruiters is to ask them how your information will be provided to companies. Due to the challenges of effectively conveying to a company the experiences that a Forces person has (as discussed in Chapter 12, on CVs), some recruiters provide their own profile to organizations rather than your own CV.

If that is the case, ask to see a copy of the profile they develop for you – firstly to check the accuracy, and also to see what you can learn from it and perhaps apply some of the elements to your own CV. Be careful how you approach this as it is more work for the recruiter, but they should be willing to provide you with this information.

Key considerations

Bear in mind the following points:

■ The industry is not regulated in many countries so you are likely to come across varying standards in terms of the recruitment agencies and the individual consultants.

■ Be clear of what you want and what you can offer.

■ Highlight your key strengths, skills, experiences etc to help the consultant sell you to the clients.

■ Get feedback on your CV, and their thoughts about interviewing, salary expectations, state of the market, and of areas for you to work on.

■ Avoid jargon – some consultants may not be specialists in your field, although I would be concerned if they didn't have a good understanding of your sector.

■ Wherever possible, get feedback on client interviews you do.

■ Don't rely solely on recruitment consultants – have recruitment as part of your own job search strategy (see Chapter 7, 'Considerations when changing career').

■ Build rapport with the consultant and stay in touch on a regular basis to keep front of mind, so you are considered for any new roles as they come in.

Key questions to ask

■ How strong is my CV?

■ What more can I do to tailor my CV for the types of roles we are discussing?

■ What is the market like currently?

■ How well do I come across?

■ What relevant roles do you currently have?

- What are my potential areas of strength and weakness?
- When was the last time you placed someone from the military?
- When did you last place someone like me and where did you place them?
- What salary could I expect with the type and level of experience I have?
- What are the next steps?

Making and maintaining contact

Recruitment consultancies will vary in how much they are going to be able to help and the relevance of the jobs they deal with, so do consider approaching a number of them for help.

The key when you are considering which ones to approach is to do your research first, get personal recommendations where possible and then shortlist a number of them to contact – five or six is a good number. Please see the Appendix for the details of some recruitment consultancies you may consider.

Something else to consider when talking to consultants is not to give the impression that your CV is with every consultant out there as they may be less inclined to help, but obviously don't lie either. Also, something that is especially common in the UK is that consultants may only contact you if they have a job brief they feel would be appropriate for you or something specific to update you on.

Therefore, please don't take it personally if you struggle to contact the consultants you are working with – the likelihood is they are working on finding you job briefs that will be of interest to you, but currently have nothing to update you on.

Final Note

My last bit of advice, and considering what I have just said it's something that can be difficult to achieve, is to build a relationship with your consultant making sure you are always front of mind. This will ensure you are one of the first people the consultant will call when they have a new relevant brief in.

Consultants are interviewing on a daily basis and you will soon slip to the back of their mind if you don't do this. Even with the sophisticated databases that a lot of agencies now use, being front of mind ensures that no briefs that are relevant to you are missed.

A note of caution though: you need to find the right balance when keeping in contact, as calling too much will begin to irritate the consultant (I know, as I ran my own recruitment consultancy!).

15

Interviewing: preparing effectively

Invitation to interviews

Something I would like to mention briefly at this point is regarding being invited in for an interview. If you are invited in for an interview, especially if it's early on in the job-hunt process and you have little experience of interviews (even if you don't think the company/role is of interest to you), my advice would be to go to the interview. The experience is going to give you some good practice of interviewing, you will be growing your network of contacts, and you could be pleasantly surprised and find the role appealing after all.

In terms of preparing effectively for interviews, below are some key points to consider. I would expect as someone trained in the Forces that you would do a lot of these things naturally, but they are certainly worth keeping front of mind.

■ **Preparation** – you can never prepare enough for an interview. Get as much information on the company as you can: new business wins; position in the marketplace; company history; key players; reputation etc.

■ **Logistics** – where are you going for the interview? How are you going to get there? Who are you going to meet? What is their position within the company? What is their background?

■ **Get there early** – there is nothing worse than being late for an interview. Plan to get there 15 minutes early. Being in reception can give you a real feel for the company, eg if you're interviewing at 7 pm and everyone is still there! Read any literature in reception that you find on the company.

■ **First impression** – first impressions count: work out what is appropriate to wear, always wear clean clothes and shoes, ironed shirt, tidy hair, brush your teeth, apply deodorant etc. Be positive, smile, have a firm handshake, look the interviewer in the eyes when you shake their hand and prepare what you are going to say... and don't waffle!

■ **Post interview** – send a thank you letter or e-mail. Review your performance – what do you feel went well and what areas might you improve on?

■ **What to say** –
  - Practise your opening and closing remarks.
  - Make sure you are focused and clear on the job you want. If you are clear, you will come across in a positive and focused way in interview. The opposite is also true – if you don't know what you want, that will come across in a negative way in interview.
  - As with your CV, consider your key relevant achievements: give examples of the main impact you've made in your roles. Practise your good-news stories.
  - Put yourself in your potential employer's shoes: what are the skills, experiences and achievements they are looking for? Match up your skills, experience and achievements where possible.

Final Note

There are three key points to highlight here:

Firstly, spend as much time as you can preparing fully before an interview. It will take longer than you think, so be aware of that.

Secondly, learn from your mistakes. Review your performance on an ongoing basis and adapt your interview technique based on what you learn.

Thirdly, prepare for rejection. Your application will more than likely get rejected from companies – it's quite normal. The key is to learn and move forwards. Wherever possible get feedback on why you didn't get the job.

16

Interview questions: how to handle them

What are the most difficult questions you could be asked? How would you answer them? Practise, practise, practise. Review your CV for insight.

Below are some examples of questions you may be asked in interview, some tips on how to answer them and some example answers to consider. Please note that the examples provided are to help you prepare your responses and may not be right for your particular situation.

- **Tell me about yourself.** A classic question to open an interview with. Don't waffle, keep your answer down to 2–3 minutes and keep it relevant – don't start talking about your science project at primary school!

- **Why did you join the Armed Forces originally?** Ensure you don't create any negative questions in the mind of the interviewer. For instance, don't say you joined up to kill people, even if you only mean it as a joke!

An example answer could be: 'I joined up because I wanted to make a difference, learn new skills and have experiences I couldn't get anywhere else.'

■ **Why are you leaving the Armed Forces?** An obvious question. Firstly, make sure you don't contradict yourself in relation to your answer to the previous question. You also need to ensure you convey the fact that you are serious about leaving the Forces, and position your views in a positive, professional manner.

An example answer could be: 'I am looking for new challenges, an opportunity to excel in the commercial world and the benefits that will come with that.'

■ **How do you think you will settle into a career in the commercial world?** The interviewer is probing around how well you will make the transition and whether you have any doubts. Reinforce all the positive aspects about working in the commercial world.

An example answer could be: 'Extremely well. I am looking forward to being stretched and challenged in new ways.'

■ **What are you going to miss the most about the Armed Forces?** Pick up on a couple of positive points about being in the Armed Forces but keep it short and succinct – don't go on and on about the positives of being in the Armed Forces otherwise the interviewer could develop doubts about you wanting to leave.

An example answer could be: 'I am going to miss the camaraderie and the opportunities to travel and experience new cultures.'

▪ **Where do you see yourself in five years time?** Make sure you convey that you are looking to progress with your career. However, don't be arrogant and don't give the impression that you may not be with the company at that point!

An example answer could be: 'I am ambitious and driven, so I would like to progress within the organization and ideally to be in xxx position within five years.' Ensure you get the right balance here and that xxx position is deemed ambitious enough but not overly ambitious!

▪ **What are your weaknesses?** A classic question and one that requires tact and thought. The key is to pick a weakness that can also be conveyed as a strength.

An example answer could be: 'I can be stubborn. It does mean though that I will always go the extra mile to achieve the desired result.'

▪ **I've just interviewed someone who has a lot of relevant experience in this industry; why should we take a chance and employ you?** This is where your research into the company and the role will come in useful – match your skills, experience and achievements with what they are looking for, giving examples. This is also your opportunity to show that you have some unique skills and experiences you can offer them, that someone who has only worked in that industry won't have.

An example answer could be: 'As part of my remit as an Army officer I have had world-leading training in leadership and have the proven ability to work in the most extreme and hostile environments. You would always be able to rely on me in a crisis situation.'

■ **Why do you want to work for this company?** Talk about the success of the company (increase in turnover and profits, share price increase, award wins, new business wins, outside perceptions of the company etc), as well as your wanting to help build on that success.

Always convey the fact that you want the job even if you are unsure you do want it – you can always decline the offer once you've been offered it.

An example answer could be: 'The company has obviously been extremely successful over the last few years and I would like to be part of that culture and help to build on that success.'

■ **How do you cope under pressure?** Make sure you have some good examples of you coping well under pressure. Being in the Armed Forces should give you lots of strong examples of working in this environment.

An example answer could be: 'I have had to make decisions in life and death situations on a number of occasions always resulting in the best possible outcome.' Give a specific example to support this if possible.

■ **You can't start with us for xx months; why should we wait and not offer the job to someone who can start much sooner?** You need to reiterate all the key skills and experiences you could bring to the company and the role, and also show that you could use the time before you started in a constructive manner, eg going on any relevant training courses, learning new skills that are required, background reading on relevant materials etc.

An example answer could be: 'I could use the extra time extremely constructively doing xxx and yyy, thereby ensuring I am hitting the ground running on day one and perfectly positioned to have a big impact on the role from the outset.'

■ **What are your salary expectations?** A potential hot potato. Don't discuss salary in a first interview unless specifically asked and always ensure you are clear on a realistic salary if you do get into a situation where you need to give a figure. However, if possible pass the question back to the interviewer and ask them what they are offering.

An example reply could be: 'Please can you tell me what you are expecting to pay someone in this role.'

■ **What questions do you have for me?** Often this question comes towards the end of an interview. Ensure you have thought of a number of questions to ask the interviewer.

Example questions could be: Where do you see the company in x years? How do you see this particular role developing? What does the performance review process entail for your staff and how frequently does it happen? What would the probationary period be?

Other questions to consider

■ **What do you know about our company?**
If you haven't done your research on the company this question will find you out! It's easy to do some research on a company so make sure you do it – you have no excuses.

■ **What would you regard as being your most significant achievement to date?**
Your answer to this question will give the interviewer some insight into what you value and what's important to you.

They could be more specific and ask what your most significant achievement is to date within work or even outside of work, so be prepared.

An example answer could be: 'That I have continued to learn and develop throughout my career and have been rewarded with a number of promotions and increased responsibility as a result.'

■ **How have you handled conflict or opposition in the past?**
This question is probing around your management and possibly your leadership skills. Give an example that shows you handling conflict with the best possible resolution. Again, I am sure with your Forces background you will be able to give some strong examples of conflict resolution.

An example answer could be: 'During my time in Iraq we had a local militia who were unhappy with our presence in the town. By highlighting the benefits we could bring to the town in terms of stability, support and resources I was able to win them over, and during the length of my tour developed a strong and lasting working relationship with them.'

■ **What difference did you make in your last job?**
Think back to the achievements you highlighted in your CV regarding your past job, and highlight them again here giving quantifiable evidence to support your achievements where possible.

■ **Describe how you motivate others**
Again, motivating others is often a key part of any role in the Armed Forces, so make sure you give a strong example.

An example answer could be: 'As part of my role I am in charge of putting new recruits through rigorous basic training. Part of that involves a weekend out in the mountains to see how they cope with lack of sleep and extremely cold temperatures. Motivation is particularly important in these types of scenarios and the recruits all commented after that particular weekend that my upbeat and positive attitude helped them to stay motivated when all they wanted to do was give up.'

▧ **What motivates you?**
Consider Table 4.2 on page 25. What were the key things that motivate you in the workplace? Reiterate them here.

An example answer could be: 'Being the best at what I do.' Give a specific example to support your answer if possible.

▧ **Describe the situation when you were last criticized at work. How did you respond?**
You need to be extremely careful how you answer this question – this could be a turning point in an interview in a negative way if you aren't careful. Similar to the 'what are your weaknesses' question, you need to convey a criticism that could be viewed as a compliment.

An example answer could be: 'My commanding officer recently told me that I was pushing myself too hard, taking on too much work and not giving myself enough down time. I took the comments on board and asked a Corporal to help me with a big project that had been taking up too much of my time. As a consequence my workload was reduced and I utilized more down time.'

▧ **What tends to demotivate you?**
Again you're looking for things that will be viewed in a positive light.

An example answer could be: 'A situation where I am not making a difference.'

■ **What is your biggest fear?**
Again, you need to ensure you are conveying the right impression.

An example answer could be: 'A fear of failure. It helps motivate me to succeed.'

■ **I would like to offer you the job now. Would you like it?**
Don't give an answer straight away! Thank them for making the offer and ask for some time to consider it. The key is to take the pressure off having to make a decision on the spot and giving yourself time to check this job is really what you want. If they are reasonable, they will understand. You can always call them back soon after the interview and accept. Please see Chapter 18, 'Evaluating job offers', for more details.

Jack's story

Jack is an existing client of mine who had a bad interview experience before we began coaching.

At the beginning of the interview Jack said things seemed to go well. He felt he had prepared well for the interview and had strong answers to all questions asked of him.

As with a lot of people in an interview situation Jack was focusing on impressing the interviewer and looking to get offered the job – he wasn't really thinking of asking questions to work out whether he actually wanted it!

In hindsight Jack told me that he didn't warm to the interviewer and that he was quite aggressive in his interview technique.

Towards the end of the interview Jack was asked what salary he was looking for and he bounced the question back, asking what they were considering for the role. Without answering, the interviewer bounced it straight back to Jack.

Jack felt uncomfortable with this and rather than directly answering took a different approach and focused on his strengths and what he could bring to the role.

The interviewer persisted and Jack eventually plucked a figure out of the air which, following research after the interview, proved to be a very high salary for that particular job. He wasn't offered the position and was initially disappointed.

The aggressive style of the interviewer was indicative of the style of the company, and once we talked this through Jack realized that he wouldn't have been suited to the role or the company anyway.

He has now decided that he will research salaries before future interviews and although he will bounce back this type of question, he will always have a figure at the back of his mind if he continues to be pushed.

He also realizes that if it happens again, then he may not be suited to that company anyway.

Final Note

If you are going to an interview soon and would like some help with preparation, make a list of possible questions and consider doing a mock interview with a friend. At the end of the interview consider what went well, and the areas you need to improve on.

If you would like some more formal and pressurized interview training with detailed feedback, then I would recommend contacting a professional such as a Career Coach for help. Please see Chapter 20 on Career Coaching for more information.

And finally (something that far too many interviewees forget): an interview is an opportunity for **both parties** to find out information so they can make a judged decision on whether there is a good match.

An interview is two-way, and although you obviously need to get the right balance, it is as much for you to get the information you need as for the other party to get the information they need.

17

Following up on job interviews

So you've had an interview, now you need to consider the possible next steps.

As soon as you can after the interview, whilst the experience is still fresh in your mind, consider the following questions and make notes:

- What went well and what can you improve on?
- What did you think of the company and the people interviewing you?
- What's your gut feel about the role?
- Are you interested in a second interview if they ask you?
- Do you feel they have any doubts about your suitability? If so, how could you alleviate those doubts if you were invited back for a second interview?
- What additional questions do you still want to ask?

Next you need to send a brief thank you e-mail to the interviewer. If there was more than one, ensure you send the e-mail to all the interviewers. An interviewer may not be the key decision maker but they may have considerable influence in deciding if you are offered the job, so cover all your bases.

Keep the thank you e-mail short and concise: thank them for the interview; reiterate that you are extremely interested in the role; maybe highlight the key reason why they should consider you, and sign off by saying you look forward to hearing from them.

18

Evaluating job offers

So you've been offered the job – congratulations! Now, do you want it? Don't let flattery or the money alone drive your decision – that could be very short-sighted and a trap that I've seen far too many people fall into. More often than not if money is the only real driver then you won't last.

Use the questions below to help gauge whether this is the right role for you.

Reaffirm what you are looking for

- **What are the skills you want to use?**
  Revisit Table 4.3 on page 26, to clarify the key skills you have and enjoy using, to help you answer this question and the question below.

- **What are the skills you want to develop?**
  As mentioned above, when answering this question

consider the skills you enjoy using and skills you want to develop.

■ **Does the role provide the challenge you are looking for and do you think it will retain your interest?**
Do you think you are going to get bored quickly in this role? If so, it is unlikely the organization is going to want to move you into a new role having just recruited you for this specific role, so what are your options? You could ask the organization to consider expanding the remit of the role to incorporate other areas of interest to you, or see if they have another role that is more appropriate; or would they consider creating a new role for you?

You also need to consider longer term whether the role is taking your career in the right direction and if it is likely to open up more opportunities for you in the future. Also, will the company/role enhance your CV?

■ **Does the role provide the level of responsibility you are looking for?**
I am not just talking about the size of a team; it could be financial responsibility, responsibility for a certain number of clients, responsibility for an area of the business, responsibility for new business etc.

■ **Are these the type of people you want to work with and for?**
This question is getting you to focus on the people. The work might be exactly what you are looking for, but are these the type of people you want to work with and for? Consider the values of the organization – what do they stand for? Compare their values to your own personal values – are the two aligned?

See the core values exercise (Table 5.1) in Chapter 5 to refresh yourself with your core values. If your values aren't aligned, it is unlikely you will be happy working in the organization long term.

■ **What are your career prospects within the company?**
Especially relevant, but something few people consider, is a company's performance. How is the company currently performing and how is it likely to perform in the future? Is the company growing and are there likely to be opportunities for you to develop and grow with the company?

If the organization is a publicly listed company, the accounts will be available for the public to view, so you can see how they are performing – both now and historically. In the UK, if the organization is a limited company, you can request this information from Companies House (www.companieshouse.gov.uk).

You obviously don't want to be in the position where you are looking to move into a more senior role in the company and have to wait for someone to leave before you can move up. Also, you don't want to be joining a company that is about to go bankrupt or needs to make redundancies – last one in, first one out and all that.

■ **What do you think you will need to do to be successful in this role?**
A key question to consider. Make a list of the top five things you think you will need to do to be successful in this role eg, increase profitability by x per cent, increase productivity of the team by x per cent, reduce overheads by £x thousand.

■ **Is the salary in the right bracket that you are looking for?**
Having discussed salary levels with the relevant recruiters, looked at salary surveys, and considered what the competition is paying for a similar role, is the salary in the right bracket for you? If it's too low, consider ways you could negotiate a higher salary – see Chapter 19 on 'Negotiating your salary' for more information.

19

Negotiating your salary

So you want the job; now to ensure you get the appropriate salary. Tread carefully, position your argument in the right way and you could end up with a better package than expected.

Some caveats

- Don't discuss salary until you are sure the employer wants you. If possible get them to open the negotiations first.
- Look at the full package not just the basic salary. If they won't move on the basic salary, are there other areas you can work on such as car allowance, guaranteed bonuses, healthcare provision, company pension scheme etc?
- Remind them of the difference you can make to the role – profitability, efficiency etc.
- Always ask for time to think about a verbal offer before accepting – don't put yourself under undue pressure.
- Use any negotiating techniques they expect you to use in the job.
- Make sure you do your research on what is an appropriate

salary for this level of role – recruiters can often help here as well as salary surveys.

■ If they won't consider offering you more money when you join the company then look to negotiate a guaranteed pay rise after your probationary period is up, or agree on a review timescale such as six months. Always ensure you have any agreement formalized in writing, and confirm dates and amounts upfront. It's very easy for the company to forget or renege on an agreement if nothing is in writing.

■ Don't take too long to give an answer – they can switch off.

Questions an employer may ask

■ **What salary are you looking for?**
As we said in Chapter 16, try not to discuss salary first. Where possible bounce the question back to them by asking what they are offering. If they persist, mention a figure at the top end of what you would accept (if not slightly higher, depending on what you think they will offer). This will then give you the opportunity to negotiate and, if necessary, to reduce the salary level you will accept.

■ **You are looking for x and the highest salary we are willing to pay is y – will you accept it?**
If you've done your research you should have a figure in mind in terms of the lowest salary you would accept. Even if this initial offer is within the parameters you would accept, if this is their first offer they could be expecting you to counter-offer so consider proposing a higher salary.

■ **You are looking for a salary above what we normally pay people at this level. Why should we pay you more?**
By asking this question, this would tell me that they are considering paying you the salary you have asked for, so highlight the key skills and experiences you can bring to the role again and see how they respond.

Final Note

Four key points to note here:

Firstly, don't be pressurized into making a decision on the spot. Give yourself time – any reasonable person will understand that you need time to think an offer through.

Secondly, make sure it is the right role for you. Sounds obvious, but don't let flattery or a particularly large salary offer sway you – consider all aspects of the job. Even if the salary is huge, if you aren't going to enjoy the job, you aren't going to end up staying.

Thirdly, don't jump at the first job opportunity that comes your way. I know it can be tempting, especially if you have been looking for a while. If you know it isn't going to be the right role for you, then discount it or consider whether it could be a stepping stone taking you in the right direction. You obviously don't want to be back looking for a new job in six months' time.

Finally, listen to your intuition. If something doesn't feel right about the job, then it probably isn't right!

20

Career Coaching

I'm going to keep this section brief, but thought you might be interested to know a little bit about Career Coaching. A lot of people don't really know what it is or how it could potentially help them.

Background

Coaching has its history in a number of disciplines from sports coaching and career counselling to therapy and business consultancy. It uses psychology-based techniques to help raise awareness and to clarify what matters most to you.

Career Coaching is about utilizing general coaching principles and techniques and applying specific career-related tools to help clarify exactly what career is going to be right for you.

It provides a confidential, objective and professional environment where you are given time to think and the tools to unravel and understand what is really important to you with your career, and what you are going to enjoy doing. Realistic goals are then set and used to help you move forward.

Regulation

Coaching in its present format is still a relatively young profession and as yet is unregulated anywhere in the world. This means that anyone can call themselves a coach, and unfortunately this means that the quality does vary considerably.

There are a number of unofficial bodies that are looking to impose some minimum standards to the profession and I have included some of the reputable ones in the Appendix. As well as giving information on the industry, courses to study etc, a number of these bodies provide lists of coaches who have trained with recognized training organizations. The lists will include coaches who specialize in a variety of fields, including Careers.

What to expect

A good career coach should be able to give you an objective view on where you are with your career, facilitate an effective programme, and provide you with the tools and techniques you need – all in a completely confidential environment.

Ultimately they should be able to help you work out what is going to be the right career for you, set a realistic action plan of how to get there, and help you to achieve it.

Also, coaches vary in their approach: at one end of the spectrum they can provide a very holistic approach to coaching, and at the other end they can be much more directive and consultative. You need to consider where on the spectrum you would like your coach to be.

Choosing the right Career Coach

Consider the following points when looking to decide on a Career Coach.

- a Career Coach with a proven track record and testimonials to support it;
- a number of years experience as a full-time coach;
- some formal training in coaching, and ideally some form of specialist training in Career Coaching;
- a member of one of the main professional coaching bodies (see Appendix);
- someone with a busy client list;
- possibly someone published, as it takes real effort and passion to put a book together;
- someone you have good rapport with and trust.

Conclusion

I hope the book has started you thinking about the many facets and most pertinent questions you need to consider in order to make a successful career transition from the Armed Forces.

There are many unique challenges that as a Forces leaver you may face, but there are also some potential advantages you have over non-military people around job hunting – make sure you make the most of them.

The Armed Forces will have taught you many skills and you will have many experiences unique to the Armed Forces that will be of interest to potential employers so make sure you communicate these effectively.

Fundamentally you can make the changes needed. You may feel this book has given you enough information to make those changes and I hope for some that this is the case. You may feel you want to do more reading, research, or even get the support of a Career Coach.

Whatever you decide to do, I hope this book has given you the incentive and motivation to start on your journey – it would be a shame if you didn't… a shame for you, that is.

As I write this, a lot of the major world economies are in financial turmoil and potentially heading for full-blown recession. You may well see this as a major barrier, preventing you from leaving the Forces. This should certainly play a part in your thinking because of the impact it will have on a lot of industries out there, but there will still be jobs available for good people who are committed and passionate.

If you have done your planning effectively and know what it is you want to do, consider the implications of the current economic climate, but don't let it stop you from achieving your goals.

Good luck.

Jon

Appendix

Armed Forces resources

UK

Ministry of Defence – www.mod.uk

Career Transition Partnership – http://www.ctp.org.uk/ctp

The Regular Forces Employment Association – www.rfea.org.uk

The Officers' Association – www.officersassociation.org.uk

Pathfinder – www.pathfinderinternational.co.uk

The List – www.thelistuk.com

Civvy Street Magazine – www.civvystreetmagazine.co.uk

Quest – www.questonline.co.uk

Recruitment Consultancies – Business Leaders (www.businessleadersuk.com), Forces Recruitment Services (www.forcesrecruitment.co.uk), Gemini Forces (www.geminiforces.com), Ex-Mil Recruitment (www.ex-mil.co.uk)

United States

Department of Defence – www.defenselink.mil

Transition Assistance Programme – www.taonline.com

Armed Forces Foundation – www.armedforcesfoundation.org

Military Officer Association of America – www.moaa.org

Other websites of interest – www.military.com, www.hireahero.org, www.recruitmilitary.com, www.hirevetsfirst.gov, www.vetjobs.com, www.militaryhire.com

The Riley Guide – http://rileyguide.com/vets.html. The Guide has a sizable list of job boards and other online career resources

Others

Canadian National Defence – www.forces.gc.ca/site/index.htm

Australian Department of Defence – www.defence.gov.au

Career Transition Assistance Scheme (Australia) – www.defence.gov.au/dsg/organisation/ctas

New Zealand Department of Defence – www.defence.govt.nz

South African Defence Department – http://www.dod.mil.za

General resources

Networking groups

Offline

BNI International – www.bni.com

Business Referral Exchange – www.brxnet.co.uk

Online

LinkedIn – www.linkedin.com

Plaxo – www.plaxo.com

Forces Reunited – www.forcesreunited.org.uk

Facebook – www.facebook.com

MySpace – www.myspace.com

Business associations

Chamber of Commerce – www.chamberofcommerce.com

Business Link – www.businesslink.gov.uk

Companies House – www.companieshouse.gov.uk

Further education

Association of MBAs – www.mbaworld.com

The Association to Advance Collegiate Schools of Business – www.aacsb.edu

Open University – www.open.ac.uk

UCAS – www.ucas.ac.uk

Myers-Briggs

For information on Myers-Briggs and help with finding a Myers-Briggs assessor – www.myersbriggs.org

Job websites

www.monster.com

www.careerbuilder.com

www.fish4jobs.co.uk/jobs

www.totaljobs.com

Counselling bodies

British Association for Counselling and Psychotherapy – www.bacp.co.uk

American Counselling Association – www.counseling.org

Coaching bodies

The International Coach Federation – www.coachfederation.org

The Association for Coaching – www.associationforcoaching.com

European Coaching Association – www.european-coaching-association.eu

Firework Career Coaching – www.fireworkcoaching.com

Industry sectors popular with Forces leavers *

Below is a list of industry sectors popular with Forces leavers as well as companies within those sectors who are historically military-friendly.

Aerospace – Honeywell (also technology, automotive), GE

Construction – NVR Inc., Jones Lang LaSalle

Defence industry – BAE Systems, Lockheed Martin, Northrop Grumman, Raytheon, Thales

Drilling – Transocean Offshore

Employment services – Manpower, Michael Page International

Engineering/manufacturing – Anheuser-Busch, Applied Materials, EG&G, ITT Corporation

Financial services – Bank of America, Barclays, Capital One Finance Corp, Morgan Stanley, Prudential, USAA

Government – CIA, FBI, Fire Service, Foreign and Commonwealth Office, MI5, MI6, Police Force

Healthcare – Health Net

Retail – Aldi, Coca-Cola, Comet, John Lewis Partnership, Marks & Spencer, Sears Holdings, Tesco, The Home Depot

Security Services – Brinks US

Technology – Booz Allen Hamilton, DynCorp International, EDS, ManTech International

Telecoms – AT&T, BT, Orange, T-Mobile

Transportation – BNSF Railway, CSX Transportation, JB Hunt Transport, Norfolk Southern, Schneider National, Southwest Airlines, Union Pacific, United Parcel Service, Werner Enterprises

Utilities/energy – Centrica, ExxonMobil (and petrochemical), GE (also finance and healthcare), Shell, Southern Company

(*List compiled from various sources, including www.gijobs. net – top 50 military-friendly employers 2007)

References

Bolles, Richard (1970, then annually) *What Colour Is Your Parachute?*, Ten Speed Press, Berkeley, CA, USA

Brown, H Jackson Jr (journalist)

Covey, S (1999) *The 7 Habits of Highly Effective People*, Simon & Schuster UK, London

Harris, Sydney J (journalist)

Hayden, Sterling (1999) *Voyage*, Sheridan House Inc, New York

Shakespeare, William (1604–5) Measure for Measure (Act 1, scene 4)

Smith, Hyrum (2000) *What Matters Most*, Simon and Schuster UK, London

Trump, Donald (entrepreneur)

UKCLC (2003) Coaching Manual (Note: UK College of Life Coaching no longer in existence)

Zeus, P and Skiffington, S (2002) *The Complete Guide to Coaching at Work*, McGraw Hill Professional, Berkshire, UK

Further reading

Career change

Barrett, J (2006) *Career, Aptitude and Selection Tests*, Kogan Page, London

Barrett, J (2008)*The Aptitude Test Workbook*, Kogan Page, London

Barrett, J (2008) *Ultimate Aptitude Tests*, Kogan Page, London

Bolles, Richard (1970, then annually) *What Colour Is Your Parachute?*, Ten Speed Press, Berkeley, CA, USA

Green, G (2003)*The Career Change Handbook*, How to Books Ltd, Oxford, UK

Lees, John (2005) *How To Get A Job You'll Love*, McGraw Hill Professional, Maidenhead, UK

Moses, Dr B (2003) *What Next?*, Dorling Kindersley Limited, London

Williams, L (2008) *Ultimate Job Search*, Kogan Page, London

Williams, N (1999) *The work we were born to do*, Element Books Limited, London

Résumé/CV

Bright, J and Earl, J (2007) *Brilliant CV – What Employers Want to See and How to Say It*, Prentice-Hall, Harlow, UK

Eggert, M (2003) *Perfect CV*, Random House Business Books, London

Perkins, G (1998) *Killer CVs and Hidden Approaches: Give Yourself an Unfair Advantage in the Executive Job Market*, Pearson Education, Harlow, UK

Williams, L (2008) *Readymade CVs*, Kogan Page, London

Williams, L (2008) *Readymade Job Search Letters*, Kogan Page, London

Yate, M (2008) *Ultimate Cover Letters*, Kogan Page, London

Yate, M (2008) *Ultimate CV*, Kogan Page, London

Interviewing

Corfield, R (2009) *Successful Interview Skills*, Kogan Page, London

Williams, L (2008) *Ultimate Interview*, Kogan Page, London

Yate, M J (2001) *Great answers to tough interview questions*, Kogan Page, London

Online applications

Chapman, A (2001) *The Monster Guide to Job Hunting*, Prentice-Hall, Harlow, UK

Career ideas

Bird, P (1999) *Dare to be different: 101 Unconventional Careers*, Hodder Arnold H&S, London

Britain's Best Employers: a Guide to the 100 Most Attractive Companies to Work For (Corporate Research Foundation), Corporate Research Foundation UK, 2005

Donald, V (1991) *Offbeat Careers: 60 Ways to Avoid Becoming an Accountant*, Kogan Page, London

Hodgson, S ed (2009) *A–Z of Careers & Jobs*, Kogan Page, London

Kent, S (2002) *Odd Jobs: Unusual Ways to Earn a Living*, Kogan Page, London

Tolley, H, Hodge, B and Tolley, C (2007) *How to Pass the New Police Selection System*, Kogan Page, London

Work/life balance

Covey, S (1999) *The 7 Habits of Highly Effective People*, Simon & Schuster UK, London

Ditzler, J (2001) *Your Best Year Yet*, Thorsons, Glasgow, UK

Parashar, F (2005) *The Balancing Act*, Simon & Schuster, UK

Self-esteem/self-confidence

Carson, R (2003) *Taming your gremlin*, HarperCollins, New York

Jeffers, S (1991) *Feel the fear and do it anyway*, Random House, London

Smith, Hyrum (2000) *What Matters Most*, Simon and Schuster, London

Tieger, Paul D and Barron-Tieger, B (2007) *Do What You Are*, Little, Brown and Company, Boston MA, USA

ALSO AVAILABLE FROM KOGAN PAGE

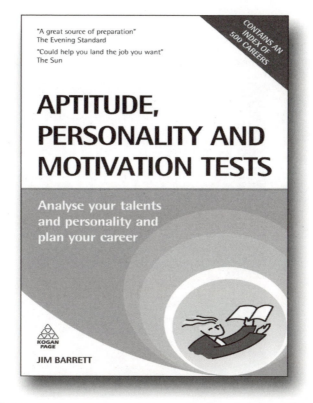

ALSO AVAILABLE FROM KOGAN PAGE

"Rebecca Corfield's step-by-step guide will make you feel more in control of the process."
Evening Standard

"Don't risk attending an interview without first reading this helpful guide."
Business Executive

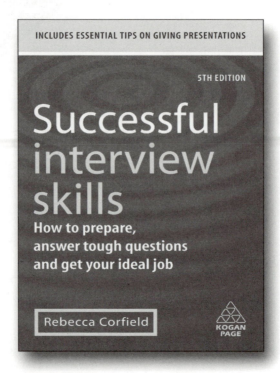

INCLUDES ESSENTIAL TIPS ON GIVING PRESENTATIONS

5TH EDITION

Successful interview skills

How to prepare, answer tough questions and get your ideal job

Rebecca Corfield

KOGAN PAGE

ISBN: 978 0 7494 5652 8   Paperback   2009

Order online now at www.koganpage.com

Sign up for regular e-mail updates on new
Kogan Page books in your interest area

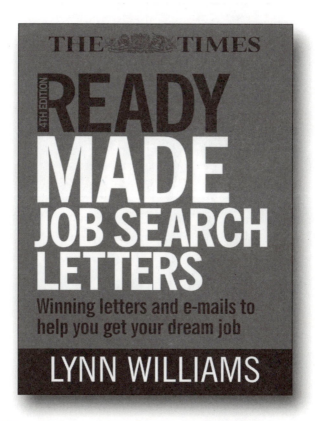

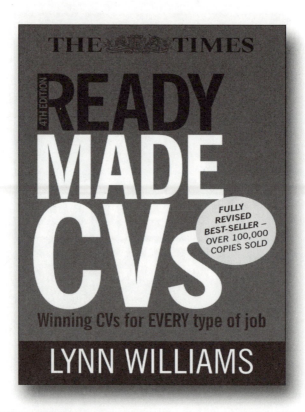